# Energy Policy, Consumer Behavior, and Solar Photovoltaic Systems in the United States



Pasha Autowala

## TABLE OF CONTENTS

## LIST OF FIGURES

## LIST OF TABLES

## LIST OF ACRONYMS

| | |
|---|---|
| AB | Assembly Bill |
| AMT | Alternative Minimum Tax |
| APN | Assessor's Parcel Number |
| ARRA | American Recovery and Reinvestment Act of 2009 |
| CARE | California Alternate Rates for Energy |
| CCSE | California Center for Sustainable Energy |
| CDD | Cooling degree days |
| CEC | California Energy Commission |
| $CO_2e$ | Carbon dioxide equivalent |
| CPUC | California Public Utilities Commission |
| CSI | California Solar Initiative |
| CZ | Climate zone |
| DC-AC | Direct current – alternating current |
| DER | Distributed energy resources |
| DF | Design factor |
| DG | Distributed generation |
| DM | Domestic Multi-Family |
| DR | Domestic Residential |
| DRLI | Domestic Residential Low-Income |
| DRSES | Domestic Residential Time-of-Use Service for Solar Electric Systems |
| DRTOU | Domestic Residential Time-of-Use |
| DSM | Demand-side management |
| EECC | Electric Energy Commodity Charge |
| EEM | Energy Efficient Mortgage |
| EPBB | Expected Performance-Based Buydown |
| ERP | Emerging Renewables Program |
| ETA | Energy Tax Act |
| EV | Electric vehicle |
| FIT | Feed-in Tariff |
| GW | Gigawatt |
| HUD | U.S. Department of Housing and Urban Development |
| kW | Kilowatt |
| kWh | Kilowatt hour |
| IEPR | Integrated Energy Policy Report |
| IOU | Investor-Owned Utility |
| IPCC | Intergovernmental Panel on Climate Change |
| ITC | Investment tax credit |
| LADWP | Los Angeles Department of Water and Power |
| LCOE | Levelized cost of energy |
| LSE | Load-serving entities |
| LTEESP | California Long-Term Energy Efficiency Strategic Plan |
| MASH | Multi-Family Affordable Solar Housing |

| | |
|---|---|
| MW | Megawatt |
| MWdc | Megawatt direct current |
| MPR | Market price referent |
| NEG | Net excess generation |
| NEM | Net energy metering |
| NOAA | National Oceanographic and Atmospheric Administration |
| NREL | National Renewable Energy Law |
| NSHP | New Solar Homes Partnership |
| PAs | Program Administrators |
| PACE | Property-Assessed Clean Energy financing |
| PBI | Performance-Based Incentive |
| PG&E | Pacific Gas & Electric |
| PPA | Power Purchase Agreement |
| PTEM | Physical-Technical-Economic Model |
| PURPA | Public Utilities Regulatory Policy Act |
| PV | Photovoltaic |
| RAM | Renewable Auction Mechanism |
| RECs | Renewable energy credits |
| RPS | Renewable Portfolio Standard |
| SAM | System Advisor Model |
| SASH | Single-family Affordable Solar Housing |
| SB | Senate Bill |
| SCE | Southern California Edison |
| SDG&E | San Diego Gas & Electric |
| SEIA | Solar Energy Industries Association |
| SGIP | Self Generation Incentive Program |
| SI | Sizing Index |
| SMUD | Sacramento Municipal Utility District |
| SoCalGas | Southern California Gas Company |
| TMY | Typical meteorological year |
| UDC | Utility Distribution Charge |
| VNEM | Virtual net energy metering |

## ACKNOWLEDGEMENTS

To Lesley: for your love, support and faith in me. Thank you!

To Nathan and Erin: for your love, patience (even if unwitting) and life-giving positive energy.

To my primary advisors during my time at Berkeley: Dick Norgaard, Dan Kammen, Sara Beckman and Alex Farrell. I will always be extremely grateful for your tremendous support, wisdom and guidance.

# Chapter 1. INTRODUCTION

## 1.1. THE RESEARCH QUESTION

This dissertation investigates adoption of solar-electric generation systems and its impacts on energy consumption in the residential sector. The study analyzes whether households in the San Diego region that installed solar systems reduced or increased their electricity consumption after system installation. The study further tests whether characteristics of the solar system, its installer, and other variables related to the property and household for which data are available, help explain changes in consumption behavior. In other words, the basic research question is "Which residential adopters increase and which decrease their consumption and why?"

The research question has clear policy relevance. Knowing more about consumer choices in the residential sector helps policymakers design and market programs to achieve savings from efficiency and encourage installation of optimally designed solar systems. Where government subsidies are available for solar systems, those resources could be most effectively allocated by encouraging that less-expensive efficiency improvements be realized prior to or in conjunction with appropriately- sized solar systems. Larger system size, if correlated with absence of observed energy consumption reductions, may indicate the existence of an inefficient subsidy, or of relative barriers that disfavor energy efficiency and conservation. As a policy matter, for a number of complementary reasons we are interested in how policy can be designed to encourage all residences, including those that install solar systems, to move in the direction of consuming less energy rather than more. Early adopters of solar systems constitute a leading demographic in the shift toward a clean energy economy, with all that entails: lower carbon emissions, postposed ratepayer-funded investment in new generation assets, domestic economic growth and the corresponding job creation, air quality benefits, and other potential positive impacts.

## 1.2. ENERGY POLICY IN THE AGE OF CLIMATE CHANGE

In the past, energy policy in the United States has been driven by the imperative to provide ever-increasing quantities of cheap and reliable energy. To the extent that energy policy sought to reduce the use of fossil fuels, such efforts by were motivated primarily by air pollution and energy security concerns (Dixon, McGowan et al. 2010). In the present age of climate change, the driving forces of energy policy are poised to change. New energy policies are being developed with the explicit goal of reducing fossil fuel use to reduce greenhouse gas (GHG) emissions (Hens, Verbeeck et al. 2001; Al-Ghandoor, Jaber et al. 2009). Scientists estimate that a 50 to 80% reduction in global GHG emissions by 2050 is likely to be necessary to prevent dangerous climate change (IPCC 2007). In the Global Warming Solutions Act of 2006, the state of California has committed to reducing its emissions to 1990 levels by 2020, and to 80% below 1990 levels by 2050. Federal laws embracing similar emission reduction targets have been considered, but not passed, by the U.S. Congress.

Households are increasingly the focus of attention in efforts to decrease GHG emissions through reduced fossil fuel consumption in the U.S. (Swan and Ugursal 2009). The residential sector accounts for 21% of U.S. energy-related carbon-dioxide emissions, including both direct fuel consumption (primarily natural gas) and household electricity usage (Energy Information Administration (EIA) 2009: 20). In California, the residential sector makes up about 14% of the state's total emissions (Consol 2008: 5-6). Addressing greenhouse gas emissions from the residential sector is critical to achieving the ambitious goals that exist in California and may exist at the national level in the future (Jones and Kammen 2011). With respect to energy consumption, the California Long-Term Energy Efficiency Strategic Plan (LTEESP) established a goal that "All cost-effective potential for energy efficiency, demand response and clean energy production will be routinely realized for all dwellings on a fully-integrated, site-specific basis." (CPUC 2008) Such integration is an ultimate long-term goal of California's energy policy, in recognition of the fact that it will be least-cost and most beneficial for customers and society as a whole.

In general, there are two broad approaches to cutting greenhouse gas emissions from energy use: saving energy by consuming less, and shifting to non-carbon based energy sources (Yalcintas and Kaya 2009). For the former, application of energy efficiency technologies and energy conservation policies are needed. The latter requires the development of alternative, non-fossil-fuel based energy sources. These strategies are complementary; indeed, to cut emissions to the degree climate scientists project as necessary, pursuing both strategies simultaneously will be required (Ekins 2004).

Energy efficiency and conservation measures have been available for many years, but still have not diffused as widely as necessary (McKenzie-Mohr, Nemiroff et al. 1995: 151; Ekins 2004: 1895). Energy efficiency improvements generally involve the use of some technology to prevent the waste of energy (Ehrhardt-Martinez and Laitner 2008). A large literature has emerged about the "barriers" or "impediments" to residential energy efficiency (Ekins 2004: 1896; Sovacool 2009: 1531). Many scholars over the years have emphasized the need to design energy efficiency measures and programs in light of the behavioral sciences (see e.g. Stern 1986; Dennis, Soderstrom et al. 1990; Stern 1992; Lutzenhiser 1994; McKenzie-Mohr, Nemiroff et al. 1995; Allcott and Mullainathan 2010). Energy conservation, in contrast, generally involves behavioral change that reduces the unnecessary use of energy (Ehrhardt-Martinez and Laitner 2008). In the modern era of energy policy and practice that dates to the mid-1970s, the focus has been on installation of increasingly efficient "widgets", independent of behavior. Since 2006, however, in the energy efficiency research and policy communities there has been a pronounced resurgence of appreciation for the importance of behavioral issues in program design (Vine 2010).

On the generation side, among alternative and renewable energy technologies, solar photovoltaic (PV) technologies hold significant potential for reducing energy-related emissions. Solar PV systems generate electricity from sunlight by means of the photoelectric effect (Jackson and Oliver 2000). Solar PV systems are typically deployed in one of two configurations: (1) large-scale systems that generate utility-scale quantities of electricity (on the order of megawatts to hundreds of megawatts), and (2) micro-generation installations, typically on building rooftops or open spaces in relatively urbanized areas, which tend to produce on the order of kilowatts (Bradford 2006). The development of a multitude of micro-generators that are connected to the grid and feed power into it allows a new vision of energy supply referred to as "distributed generation" (DG) or "distributed energy resources" (DER).

The first part of this section reviews federal and state policies for residential solar PV. The solar-PV households included in this study have been and remain subject to these policies. The second part discusses how solar-PV and energy efficiency policies have often run on separate but parallel tracks and how greater coordination between them would improve program and policy outcomes.

### 1.3. General Policy Framework for Solar-PV

From 2005 to 2009, the amount of electricity produced from solar PV nationally grew by one-third.[1] Since the 1970s, both the federal government and state governments have developed policies to encourage renewable energy in the residential sector. Among states, California has been a clear leader (Energy Information Administration (EIA) 2005; Geller, Harrington et al. 2006: 568; Laitner, Ehrhardt-Martinez et al. 2009); further, the San Diego, San Francisco Bay Area and Los Angeles regions have been leaders within the state and, by extension, nationally (Davis, Madsen et al. 2012). This section summarizes the evolution of both the federal and California policy frameworks.

#### 1.3.1. Federal Policy

Federal incentives for residential solar began with the National Energy Act of 1978 and the associated Public Utilities Regulatory Policy Act (PURPA) and Energy Tax Act (ETA). PURPA was designed to create a level playing field for nonutility producers of renewable energy as well as create incentives for large utilities to invest in renewable energy. It marked the first time that individuals had the legal right to be paid a fair market price for the excess electricity generated by their PV system (Hinman 2008-2009). PURPA required public utilities to purchase power from qualifying third parties and capped the rate paid at the utility's "avoided cost." Results of the implementation varied from state to state, with California producing the most favorable results (Martinot, Wiser et al. 2005).

The Energy Tax Act encouraged homeowners to invest in energy conservation and solar technology through tax credits. A federal energy tax credit of up to $2,000, 15% for basic weatherization measures and 40% for solar space and water heating (solar electric was not commercially available at that time) was given for devices installed on people's homes between April 20, 1977 and January 1, 1986 (CEC 2010). The Tax Reform Act of 1986 then called for it to be phased out, and in January of 1987, the credit fell to 12%. It was reduced to 10% to following year and remained at this level until 2005.

The Energy Policy Act of 1992 gave relatively little attention to renewable energy, but it did help enable the development of the Energy Efficient Mortgage (EEM) through which borrowers could qualify for more expensive but energy efficient homes or include the cost of energy improvements (including solar PV) into their mortgages without additional credit assessments. A five-state pilot program expanded to ten states in 1994, and became available nationally in 1995. However, use of the EEM has been very low; only 1,100 EEMs were approved by the U.S. Department of Housing and Urban Development (HUD) nationwide in 2007 (Caruthers 2009), and uptake has not accelerated notably since then. The modest penetration of EEMs reflects the onerous application process, the fact that they are not well-known, the fact that significant due diligence is required on the front-end to prove

---

[1] Calculated from data in EIA, Table 3: Electricity Net Generation from Renewable Energy by Energy Use Sector and Energy Source, 2005 – 2009, available at http://www.eia.gov/cneaf/solar.renewables/page/table3.pdf.

the effectiveness of the measures proposed, and the limited range of measures permitted for the incremental financing that the EEM provides. Indeed a very similar set of barriers exist for other integrated whole-home energy efficiency programs being developed and implemented across the nation (Wilson-Wright 2007; Fuller, Kunkel et al. 2010).

Federal policies to subsidize residential installations of grid-connected PV systems increased markedly in the 2000s. The Energy Policy Act of 2005 created the Residential Energy-Efficient Property Credit, providing a federal tax credit for installation of solar photovoltaic systems, solar water heating systems, and fuel cells. This financial incentive allowed homeowners a 30% tax credit, up to $2,000, for purchase and installation of a residential solar system. The Tax Relief and Health Care Act of 2006 extended the credit through the end of 2008, and the Emergency Economic Stabilization Act of 2008 extended it for another eight years (SEIA 2010).

The American Recovery and Reinvestment Act of 2009 (ARRA) eliminated the $2,000 cap on the credit for residential systems, providing residential installations the same full 30% credit already applicable to non-residential installations. Thus, beginning with tax year 2009, homeowners with sufficient tax liability were able to claim significantly higher credit. This change may have impacted homeowner decision making, and thus residential system uptake, and so is relevant for our analysis. The change applies for systems installed from January 1, 2009 until December 31, 2016, may only be applied for the taxpayer's principal residence, and may be applied to existing homes as well as new construction.[2]

### 1.3.2. California State Policy

In California, policies that support residential solar-PV installations fall into two categories: direct incentives for installations, and policies supporting the generation and use of energy from them. After discussion of these policies, this section summarizes the extent to which these policies have been successful as measured by the number of systems installed.

The California state entities most responsible for making and implementing state energy policies are the California Energy Commission (CEC), the state's primary energy policy and planning agency, and the California Public Utilities Commission (CPUC), which regulates privately-owned electric and natural gas companies as well as telecommunications, water, railroad, rail transit, and passenger transportation companies. California is currently served by 75 retail electric utility companies, also called load serving entities (LSEs).[3] Of the 75 LSE's in California, six are investor-owned utilities (IOUs); 48 are publicly owned utilities; four are rural electricity cooperatives; three are Native American utilities; and the last 14 fit into the "other" category. The five largest electric utilities are: Southern California Edison (SCE), Pacific Gas & Electric (PG&E), Los Angeles Department of Water and Power (LADWP), San Diego Gas & Electric (SDG&E), and Sacramento Municipal Utility District (SMUD). Together these entities provide electric service to around 95% of the homes and businesses in the state.

---

[2] EPA, Energy Star, Federal Tax Credits for Consumer Energy Efficiency, http://www.energystar.gov/index.cfm?c=tax_credits.tx_index.

[3] CEC, California Electricity Sector Overview, http://www.energyalmanac.ca.gov/electricity/overview.html

Direct Incentives for System Installations

California began creating incentives for residential solar in the late 1990s. Assembly Bill (AB) 1890 (1996) deregulated the state's investor-owned electric utilities and create incentives for grid-tied PV systems. Following this deregulation, the CEC instituted a new Renewable Energy Program to provide financial incentives to support existing, new, and emerging renewable resources. In 1998, the CEC created the Emerging Renewables Program (ERP) to provide rebates and production incentives to residential and small commercial utility consumers who purchased and installed renewable energy technologies for on-site generation, including solar photovoltaic systems. To qualify for ERP incentives, PV system size was limited to 30 kilowatts (kW). Within the large IOU service territories, systems larger than 30 kW were covered under the Self Generation Incentive Program (SGIP), established in 2001 by the CPUC. In 2002, Senate Bill (SB) 1038 was passed and called for the Emerging Renewables Program to be extended through 2006. The program was again extended through 2011, by SB 1250 and SB 107, both signed into law in 2006; however, this extension limited the ERP to non-solar technologies, in deference to the concurrent development of the California Solar Initiative (CSI), described below.

In 2001, during the California electricity crisis, a solar tax credit was created by SB 17X. The credit, for tax years 2001-2003, was equal to the lesser of 50% of the net purchase cost of a photovoltaic with a generating capacity of between 10 and 200 kilowatts, or a fixed credit of $2.50 per watt of installed capacity. The law allowed credit for one system per each separate legal parcel of property or per each address of the taxpayer in California. The credit was reduced to $1.25 per watt for tax years 2004-2005 and ended on January 1, 2006. Also, Section 73 of the California Revenue and Taxation Code allows a property tax exemption for certain types of solar energy systems (photovoltaics systems are eligible) installed between January 1, 1999, and December 31, 2016. This incentive is available to commercial, industrial and residential sectors and allows for 100% of the system's cost to be excluded from assessed property value.

In 2006, the CSI was created, transferring the solar energy rebate program for existing homes from the CEC to a ratepayer-funded effort administered by three regional program administrators (PAs): PG&E and SCE in their respective service territories, and the California Center for Sustainable Energy (CCSE) in SDG&E territory. The new effort was funded by ratepayers through an adder to the energy procurement charge on each non-low-income electricity bill, according to specifics defined in a series of decisions by the CPUC, in rulemakings R. 06-03-004 and R. 10-05-004. At the same time, rebates for PV systems over 30kW were transferred from the SGIP to the CSI program.

Since 2007, then, the CSI constitutes the state's core incentive program for all behind-the-meter PV systems, whether residential or non-residential. Originally, the CSI was a CPUC initiative and thus the rebate was to be limited to customers of the state's three investor-owned electric utilities. However, the legislature became involved and developed SB 1 which expanded the program to include the municipal territories as well, and placed additional requirements on the CSI in the IOU territories. Among the more relevant SB1 terms for our purposes here is SB1's direction that the CEC develop eligibility guidelines for the CSI program—guidelines that would likely require energy efficiency measures during or prior to the installation of solar. Including the New Solar Homes Partnership described below, the CSI rebate program has a budget of $3.2 billion over ten years with the objective of providing 3,000 megawatts (MW) of solar capacity by 2016 (CPUC 2006).

The incentive structure of the CSI is more complex than previous solar incentive programs. The CPUC had as its explicit goal the transformation of the distributed solar marketplace, such that after the program's end (estimated at 2016), the market for small-scale solar would be able to persist and grow without further subsidies. In keeping with this market-based approach, and explicitly stated in SB1, the program incentive structure was intended to reward system performance. These policy directives and subsequent program stipulations resulted in a unique program design.

First, incentives are paid in one of two ways: up front or over time. Smaller systems may receive an up-front, one-time incentive while larger systems must be paid over time based on actual energy production. Specifically, systems under a specified size (initially 100kW, subsequently reduced to 50kW and finally to 30kW) may receive a lump sum Expected Performance-Based Buydown (EPBB). EPBB incentives are awarded as a one-time, up-front payment based on expected performance, which is calculated using equipment ratings and installation factors such as geographic location, system orientation, mounting method and actual shading present on the modules at the site. The maximum EPBB payment is adjusted downward by a design factor (DF) based on modeling with a PV calculator tool that compares actual installation details to those of an optimally-installed fixed-mounted model system. For the 5,243 residential PV systems included in the present study, all of which were installed in the San Diego region between January 2007 and December 2010, CSI design factors ranged from 1.17 to 0.69, with an overall average of 0.97; however, a DF greater than 1 (i.e. a tracking system) does not result in an increased EPBB incentive.

Second, incentive levels decline over time as the aggregate capacity of PV installations increases. Declining incentives are a reflection of the legislature's intent that CSI result in a self-supporting solar marketplace; SB1 required a minimum annual reduction in incentive levels of 7%. In implementation of SB1, the CPUC operationalized this mandate using 10 incentive levels, each with a predefined total installed capacity. Early incentive "steps" had small capacity and higher incentive rates; latter steps more capacity and progressively lower incentives. The EPBB incentive began in January 2007 at $2.50/W for residential systems and has been adjusted downward periodically based on the program's cumulative capacity of the systems installed. Performance-Based Incentives (PBI) were initially set at a rate of $0.39/kWh for the first five years for taxable entities (residential included). The incentives are paid monthly based on the actual energy produced, for a period of five years. Residential and small commercial projects under the 30 kW threshold have the option of receiving either EPBB or PBI, however, all installations of 30 kW or larger must receive PBI. For both EPBB and PBI systems, government and nonprofit organizations receive a slightly more favorable rate to compensate for their lack of access to the federal tax credit. The CSI incentive structure is shown in Table 1.1.

**Table 1.1. CSI Steps - Capacity Buckets and Incentive Levels**

| Step | MW in Step | | EPBB Payments (per Watt) | | | PBI Payments (per kWh) | | |
|---|---|---|---|---|---|---|---|---|
| | | | Residential | Non-Residential | | Residential | Non-Residential | |
| | San Diego | Statewide* | | Commercial | Government/ Non-Profit | | Commercial | Government/ Non-Profit |
| 1 | -- | 50 | n/a | n/a | n/a | n/a | n/a | n/a |
| 2 | 7.2 | 70 | $2.50 | $2.50 | $3.25 | $0.39 | $0.39 | $0.50 |
| 3 | 10.3 | 100 | $2.20 | $2.20 | $2.95 | $0.34 | $0.34 | $0.46 |
| 4 | 13.4 | 130 | $1.90 | $1.90 | $2.65 | $0.26 | $0.26 | $0.37 |
| 5 | 16.4 | 160 | $1.55 | $1.55 | $2.30 | $0.22 | $0.22 | $0.32 |
| 6 | 19.6 | 190 | $1.10 | $1.10 | $1.85 | $0.15 | $0.15 | $0.26 |
| 7 | 22.1 | 215 | $0.65 | $0.65 | $1.40 | $0.09 | $0.09 | $0.19 |
| 8 | 25.8 | 250 | $0.35 | $0.35 | $1.10 | $0.05 | $0.05 | $0.15 |
| 9 | 29.4 | 285 | $0.25 | $0.25 | $0.90 | $0.03 | $0.03 | $0.12 |
| 10 | 36.1 | 350 | $0.20 | $0.20 | $0.70 | $0.03 | $0.03 | $0.10 |
| | **180.3** | **1800** | * Step 1 is carryover from the Self-Generation Incentive Program, and is not part of the CSI program. | | | | | |

*Source: CPUC Decision 06-12-033, 12/18/2006.*

In addition to the two rebates discussed above, 10% of the CSI Program budget ($216 million) has been allocated to two low-income solar rebate programs: the Single Family Affordable Solar Housing (SASH) program and the Multi-Family Affordable Housing (MASH) program. The MASH program is administered by the same PAs as the general market CSI; the SASH program is administered statewide by Grid Alternatives under contract to SCE, with the actual costs for the program shared proportionally by SCE, PG&E and SDG&E. MASH and SASH each has a budget of $108 million. As required by the CPUC, the utilities have developed virtual net energy metering (VNEM) tariffs which allow MASH participants to allocate the kWh credits from a single solar system across multiple electric accounts at the same building complex.

Solar on newly-constructed buildings has also been the subject of California program efforts. Beginning in 2007, the CEC began managing its New Solar Homes Partnership (NSHP) program. The NSHP provides financial incentives and other support to home builders and encourages the new construction of energy efficient solar homes.[4] The NSHP is funded with $400 million allocated to the CEC between 2007 and 2012. The NSHP specifically targets market-rate and affordable single-family and multifamily sectors, with the goal of achieving 400 MW of installed solar electric capacity on new homes, and to have solar electric systems on 50% of all new homes built in California by the end of 2016. Incentives are determined by the housing type and the expected performance of the system, which depends on factors like equipment efficiency, geographic location, orientation, tilt, shading, and time-dependent valuation. To qualify for incentives, the residential dwelling unit must achieve at least 15% higher energy efficiency than the current Title 24 Building Energy Efficiency Standards (CEC 2010).

Most recently, California governor Jerry Brown has announced and begun strategic planning for a 12 GW DG goal for the state by 2020. At least 3 GW are expected to come from small-scale solar energy systems, which represents a 50% increase over the CSI/NSHP goals for 2016. While the particular post-CSI initiatives to support this increased solar generation goal have yet to be determined as of this writing, it seems clear that questions of program best practices, cost-effectiveness and the behavior of solar adopters will continue to be an important part of the discussion.

---

[4] CEC & CPUC, Go Solar California: What Is The New Solar Homes Partnership? http://www.gosolarcalifornia.ca.gov/about/nshp.php

Net Energy Metering

In addition to direct incentives for the installation of systems, California policy has been developed to enable small (under 1 MW) solar and other distributed renewable generators to install and operate these systems cost-effectively. In particular, net energy metering (NEM) provides significant direct benefits to the owners or host customers of distributed generation systems. NEM measures the difference between the electricity a homeowner buys from a utility and the electricity a solar system generates and feeds back to the electric grid over a 12-month period. The meter keeps track of the net difference as the PV system generates electricity or uses electricity from the transmission grid. California's NEM law, which took effect in 1996, requires the state's utilities, with the exception of the LADWP, to offer NEM to all customers for solar and wind-energy systems up to 1 MW.[5] Investor owned-utilities have the additional requirement of offering NEM for biogas-electric systems and fuel cells.

Originally, the law applied to wind systems, solar-electric systems and hybrid (wind/solar) systems, but AB 2228 (2002) allowed biogas-electric facilities up to 1 MW to net meter under a pilot program that would expire December 31, 2005. The pilot program was later extended until December 31, 2009. The overwhelming majority of solar PV customer-generators choose to be on a net NEM tariff.[6] In December 2010 there were over 75,000 residential and non-residential accounts enrolled in California's NEM programs. The current study examines in detail 5,243 of these customers in the San Diego region.

For systems producing more electricity than is consumed on-site, the "net excess generation" (NEG) is carried forward to the customer's next bill; historically any NEG remaining at the end of each 12-month period belonged to the customer's utility, without compensation to the customer. However, AB 920 was signed into law on October 11, 2009. Implemented by the CPUC in 2011, AB 920 requires electric distribution utilities and cooperatives to compensate eligible NEM customers for electricity produced in excess of on-site load over a 12-month period. The law stipulates that utilities must have informed their NEM customers, by January 31, 2010, that they are eligible for net surplus compensation, and it directed the CPUC to establish, by January 1, 2011, a net surplus compensation rate to be paid to those who produce more energy than they consume in a 12-month period.[7] The utility companies can either provide direct payment to the customer-generators or credit the customer to offset any future electricity bills. All systems within the present study (installed prior to 2011) are in the historical situation: NEG was not in practice being purchased by their respective utility. However, 2010 solar adopters might have expected that it would be in the future.

---

[5] See California Public Utilities Code Section 2821-2829. The exemption applies to "local publicly owned electric utility that serves more than 750,000 customers and that also conveys water to its customers." The only utility in the state meeting these criteria is LADWP.

[6] CPUC, Net Energy Metering (NEM), http://www.cpuc.ca.gov/PUC/energy/DistGen/netmetering.htm.

[7] AB No. 920 (October 11, 2009), available at http://www.leginfo.ca.gov/pub/09-10/bill/asm/ab_0901-0950/ab_920_bill_20091011_chaptered.pdf .

Non-NEM Distributed Solar Electricity Procurement

Two new electricity procurement approaches are beginning to share the distributed solar space with NEM. These upcoming initiatives are the Feed-in Tariff (FIT) and the Renewable Auction Mechanism (RAM).

SB 32 (2009) directs the CPUC to create a California FIT, for systems up to 5 MW and covering up to 750 MW across the IOU service territories. Still under development by the CPUC in 2012, the FIT may complement NEM and incentive programs well, and may enable a new sector of the DER marketplace. Under a FIT, a utility or third-party owns a PV system, injects the power into the grid directly (not behind the meter), and receives payment from the utility, typically a flat per-kWh rate. A FIT is generally more transparent than NEM, since the payment is easily calculable as opposed to NEM under which the value of energy generated by the system depends on the retail rate.

The Renewable Auction Mechanism (RAM) is a newer program to facilitate procurement from larger renewable DG systems, ranging from 3 MW to 20 MW. [8] The IOUs are authorized to procure a total of 1,299 MW through RAM by holding four simultaneous reverse auctions over two years. [9] In the auctions, IOUs select projects based on viability and price until their capacity limit for that auction is reached. As explained by the CPUC, RAM "allows bidders to set their own price, provides a simple standard contract for each utility, and allows all projects to be submitted to the CPUC through an expedited regulatory review process."[10]

The expanded and increasingly diverse clean energy "ecosystem" requires careful attention in order to reap the maximum harvest: as these markets grow, evolve and specialize, both existing practices and new approaches are needed to nurture the various distinct segments. Comprehensiveness, fairness and transparency should be core elements of an inclusive approach. The goal is to ensure that the appropriate distributed resources are deployed where they provide highest public benefit and most effectively utilize public and/or ratepayer resources.

Wholesale Renewable Procurement: Renewable Portfolio Standards

As of 2009, 26 U.S. states and Washington, DC have mandatory Renewable Portfolio Standards (RPS), which require that a fixed percentage of a utility's retail sales be supplied by renewable energy sources.[11] Established in 2002 under SB 1078, California's

---

[8] CPUC Decision (D.) 10-12-048 (December 16, 2010), available at http://docs.cpuc.ca.gov/word_pdf/FINAL_DECISION/128432.pdf

[9] The procurement limit was expanded from 1000 MW to 1299 MW by CEC Decisions D.12-02-035 (February 16, 2012), available at http://docs.cpuc.ca.gov/word_pdf/FINAL_DECISION/160210.pdf, and D.12-020-02 (February 1, 2012).

[10] CPUC, Renewable Auction Mechanism, http://www.cpuc.ca.gov/PUC/energy/Renewables/hot/Renewable+Auction+Mechanism.htm

[11] DSIRE, Database of State ncentives for Renewables and Efficiency, www.dsireusa.org.

RPS is one of the most ambitious renewable energy standards in the United States, originally requiring 20% renewable energy by 2017.[12] In 2003, the Energy Action Plan I accelerated the 20% deadline to 2010; and in 2006, the accelerated deadline was codified in SB 107. An executive order then required that the percentage be raised to 33% by 2020 and after three legislative efforts in as many years, this higher goal became law with the governor's signing of SB 2X in 2011.

The CPUC and the CEC jointly implement the RPS program. The CPUC reports quarterly to the state legislature on the progress of IOUs toward meeting their RPS goals. The CPUC is also responsible for determining annual procurement targets and enforcing compliance; reviewing and approving each IOU's renewable energy procurement plan; reviewing IOU contracts for RPS-eligible energy; establishing the standard terms and conditions used by IOUs in their contracts for eligible renewable energy; and calculating market price referents (MPRs) for non-renewable energy that serve as benchmarks for the price of renewable energy.

The CEC's responsibilities are twofold. It must certify that the eligible renewable resources meet the criteria contained in the bill, as well as design and implement a tracking and verification system.[13] This system ensures that renewable energy output is counted only once for the purpose of the RPS and assists in verifying retail product claims.

### 1.4. Residential Solar-PV Installations in the U.S., California and San Diego

PV installation has grown at rates in the high double-digits since 2005. In 2010 over 250 MWdc of residential solar PV was installed in the U.S., almost ten times the amount installed in 2005 (SEIA 2011).

With favorable state policies, solar-PV finds itself on a steep adoption curve in California. According to statistics compiled by the California Energy Commission, the generation of energy by solar-PV systems has grown quickly, particularly since the establishment of the California Solar Initiative in 2007. In 2000, there were just 238 customer-sited solar projects installed in California's investor owned utility territories. By the end of 2006, there were 22,346 such solar projects. By the end of 2010, the number more than tripled to 77,461 customer-sited solar projects in the IOU territories (CPUC 2011: 21 tbl. 3). In terms of the capacity of these systems, at the close of 2006, there were 165 MW of solar capacity installed; capacity more than quadrupled to 746 MW by the end of 2010 (CPUC 2011). California accounts for around 49% of the nation's PV installations and capacity (Sherwood 2010).

As of December 2010, the City of San Diego had the highest number of small-scale solar-PV installations of any city in California (and by extension of any city in the entire U.S.), as well as the greatest MW capacity of such systems (Madsen, Kinman et al. 2011). This leadership continued into 2012 (Davis, Madsen et al. 2012); San Diego's solar marketplace is arguably the most robust in the country. At the end of 2011 there were 85 MW of NEM PV systems within SDG&E service territory, an area which covers all of San

---

[12] CPUC, California Renewable Portfolio Standard (RPS), http://www.cpuc.ca.gov/PUC/energy/Renewables.

[13] CEC, Renewables Portfolio Standards (RPS) Proceeding Docket #11-RPS-01 and 03-RPS-1078, http://www.energy.ca.gov/portfolio/*index.html.

Diego County and a portion of southern Orange County. 60% of the United States' residential PV installations are located in California (SEIA 2011); the San Diego region alone accounts for a full 5% of the nationwide total. At the end of 2011, California's solar industry involved 3,500 firms directly employing over 25,000 workers (Madsen, Kinman et al. 2011: 17). In the San Diego region the small-scale solar industry has grown from 80 participating contractors in 2007 to over 250 at the end of 2010.[14]

Figure 1.1 shows the cumulative capacity of NEM solar system in SDG&E territory from its functional beginning 1999 (when there were only 6 grid-connected PV systems installed) through September 2011.

**Figure 1.1. NEM PV Capacity in SDG&E Territory (09/2011)**

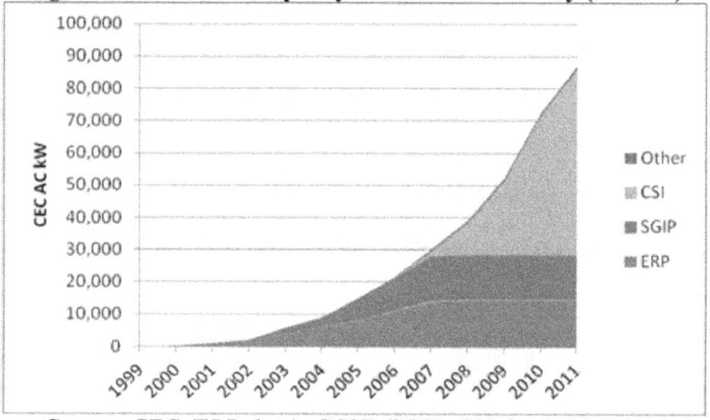


*Source: CEC (ERP data); CCSE (SGIP, CSI data); SDG&E (other)*

Prior to 2007, the incentive programs supporting NEM PV were the Emerging Renewables Program (ERP) and the Self-Generation Incentive Program (SGIP). The ERP was administered statewide by the CEC and covered PV system smaller than 10 kW; the SGIP funded PV systems larger than 10 kW, and was administered regionally by the PG&E, SCE and CCSE. The CSI rolled all PV support into one program, and adopted the SGIP's administrative structure.

PV installations are dispersed across the region. Roughly equal numbers of systems are installed along the temperate coast and inland areas. This geographic diversity is interesting for our purposes here, since energy consumption drivers, and the potential for rebound, will most certainly vary by climate.

### 1.5. The Coordination of Solar and Energy Efficiency

Policies to promote renewable energy generation and policies to promote energy efficiency have historically not been well coordinated. Rather, as described by Prindle et al. (2007), these "twin pillars of sustainable energy" have generally been pursued on "separate tracks." This section describes how renewable energy and energy efficiency policies

[14] California Solar Initiative (CSI) data, California Center for Sustainable Energy (CCSE).

relevant to the residential sector have interacted in the past and makes some preliminary observations about how they might be more strategically integrated in the future.

Solar energy and energy efficiency policies have typically been pursued side-by-side, with little integration. Like the first federal policies supporting renewable energy development, the first federal initiatives in the area of residential energy efficiency came in the 1970s. The Energy Policy and Conservation Act of 1975 sought to address rising energy prices and imports through encouraging energy efficiency and conservation (Dixon, McGowan et al. 2010). Guided by this and other federal and state laws in the late 1970s, energy efficiency programs (demand-side management, or DSM) came to be viewed as a source of new electricity supply that could be evaluated for cost-effectiveness just like proposed power generation facilities (supply-side management). In the 1980s, regulators began to require that utilities implement integrated resource planning (IRP, also called "least-cost" planning), which identified both potential power acquisitions and potential conservation measures. Increasing levels of funding for DSM resulted as efficiency measures were often chosen instead of or in combination with new power generation acquisitions based on their greater cost-effectiveness. Funding for utility DSM peaked at around $2.4 billion in 1993 (Levine, Koomey et al. 1995; Gillingham, Newell et al. 2004: 17).

By the late 1990s, a wave of retail electricity deregulation had arrived and the prospects dimmed for funding of utility DSM programs (Dixon, McGowan et al. 2010: 21). Integrated resource plans were largely rendered irrelevant as cost reduction reigned, and investments in energy efficiency declined markedly. However, in the mid-2000s, after the California energy crisis demonstrated some of the weaknesses of the market approach, utilities and their regulators in many ways returned to IRP, now enhanced by the addition of criteria such as environmental and health considerations (e.g. $CO_2$ and mercury emissions) and cost stability (e.g. preventing overreliance on price-volatile resources such as hydro and natural gas) to complement the traditional cost-effectiveness criteria.

In addition, after DSM spending plummeted in the mid to late 1990s, state regulators began to establish so-called public benefit funds (PBF), which are typically funded by a per-kWh charge on the state regulated electricity distribution system (Gillingham, Newell et al. 2004: 22). PBFs have commonly been used to support energy efficiency programs, renewable energy programs and programs to assist low-income families pay their energy bills. With these changes, utility DSM spending began to rise again in the 2000s (Gillingham, Newell et al. 2004: 22). In California, the utilities currently collect roughly $1 billion annually (CPUC 2011), on average, in PBF and similarly-targeted procurement funds; these resources have funded a wide variety of mainly energy efficiency programs, but also some efforts to develop and promote renewable energy, such as solar energy R&D and application of PV and solar-thermal technologies in new construction. Around 10-15%, or an average of about $100 million per year in PBFs, have been invested in renewable energy efforts, and of this around 50% has focused on solar-PV (Adi Kuduk and Anders 2006; CPUC 2011).

Also in the 2000s, federal tax credits were established for energy efficiency in the same federal laws that established tax credits for renewable energy development. The Energy Policy Act of 2005 created a homeowner tax credit of 10% on the purchase of qualified insulation systems, exterior windows and doors, and metal roofs. The maximum credit that could be taken for all taxable years (2005 through 2007) was $500. After expiring in 2007, the tax credit was extended and expanded by the Energy Improvement and Extension Act of 2008 and ARRA. The enhanced credit applies across a broader range of energy efficiency improvements, and increased the homeowner credit to 30% of the cost, up to $1,500, for equipment installed during the two-year period of 2009 and 2010. In 2010 these credits were modified for 2011 back to the original, reduced levels.

As with renewable energy development, California has been a policy leader in promoting household energy efficiency. The 1974 Warren-Alquist State Energy Resources Conservation and Development Act created the California Energy Commission (CEC) to be the state's principal energy policy and planning organization. The CEC's responsibilities included power plant siting and licensing; forecasting energy supply and demand; developing energy efficiency standards for; and technology development (Hanemann 2008: 123). With its new authority, the CEC developed rigorous appliance and building efficiency standards, exceeding the efforts of the federal government and other states. In the 1980s and 1990s, the CPUC also contributed to energy efficiency adoption by using its regulatory powers to motivate the investor-owned utilities to implement energy efficiency programs (Geller, Harrington et al. 2006: 569). As a result of these and other complementary efforts including stringent efficiency codes for new construction (Title 24) and tightened appliance standards (Title 20), California's electricity consumption per capita remained flat between 1975 and 2005, even while it grew by 50% over the same period nationally (Hanemann 2008: 123).

In some ways, it is understandable and appropriate to manage parallel policy tracks for renewable energy and energy efficiency. Renewable energy development and energy efficiency adoption are unique activities with different supply and demand dynamics. As foci of market transformation policy, each area logically required a set of activities and incentives tailored to the needs of its particular stakeholders, economics, etc. Combining the two in ways that presented barriers to either could have undermined the primary policy goals. Yet there are compelling reasons to move towards greater integration. In the residential sector, for example the "adopter" of each is usually the same entity—the homeowner—and the presence of separate energy efficiency and renewable energy support efforts is, from his/her perspective, an artificial program construct. Indeed, both energy efficiency and renewable energy are needed for any project taking a "zero-energy" approach. Thus from a policy perspective, we are interested in the effectiveness of not only individual programs, but also the ways in which the various program offerings interact, in the context of most effectively influencing customer behaviour, whether for energy savings, peak reduction, carbon savings or other relevant long-term goals. Effective policy coordination could potentially enhance penetration of each, or at a minimum provide necessary support and programmatic flexibility such that customers who so desire may easily do integrated, aggressive clean energy upgrades.

In the early 2000s, the CEC began to recognize the possibility of and need for coordination between energy efficiency and renewable energy policy in the state. In 2005, the CEC and CPUC adopted an Energy Action Plan that set forth a priority sequence (or "loading order") for actions to address increasing energy needs (CEC and CPUC 2005: 2). Under it, energy efficiency and demand response are the state's preferred means of meeting electricity resource needs, followed by renewable generation, and finally clean and efficient fossil-fired generation.

With respect to new building construction, coordination between energy efficiency and distributed generation is relatively straightforward. In the mid-2000s, California began to develop policies centering on the notion of zero-net-energy homes, which require combined deployment of renewable energy and advanced energy efficiency technologies (Prindle, Eldridge et al. 2007). The CEC's 2007 Integrated Energy Policy Report recommended adjusting the state's energy standard to require net-zero energy performance in newly-constructed residential buildings by 2020, and in new commercial buildings by 2030 (Rawlins and Paterson 2010). The CEC's 2012 Integrated Energy Policy Report Update maintains the CEC's traditional emphasis on energy efficiency but also, in the context of the California governor's 12 GW Challenge, focuses on scaling up distributed renewable generation.[15]

With respect to existing buildings, however, the perceived tension between solar and energy efficiency remains much less resolved. The tension is evident, for example, in the context of the parallel, and entirely separate, developments of the CSI's energy efficiency guidelines and the CPUC's 2008-2010 energy efficiency program portfolio. Programmatically, energy efficiency and renewable energy programs have operated largely in siloes. There is some limited evidence that the benefits of integration are being recognized by the CPUC and CEC. In practice, there is some linkage in the marketplace at the consumer level—in the form of contractors who work in both areas—but the complexity and lack of integration of the programmatic supports do not facilitate the sale and implementation process for either efficiency or PV projects, and certainly does not encourage their integration.

Most relevant to this dissertation is the question of whether residences that receive subsidies to install PV systems should be required to previously or simultaneously attain a certain degree of energy efficiency, for example through the installation of efficiency measures that are more cost-effective than PV. The CSI, established in 2007, required that before installing a PV system, households conduct an energy audit.[16] The CEC initially expressed its interest in requiring that all cost-effective energy efficiency improvements actually be made prior to or in conjunction with installation of PV. After hearing substantial protest from solar industry groups, the CEC pulled back to a much less onerous position, requiring a relatively pro-forma energy assessment at participating facilities.

This change in policy highlights the differing views among California stakeholder on this issue. While it may be clear that greater efficiency and new non-fossil based energy supplies are both part of the solution to reducing greenhouse gas emissions associated with the residential sector, the question of how to coordinate them is difficult. Minimal detailed knowledge exists regarding whether and how residences choose to coordinate energy efficiency and renewable energy installation in practice. This dissertation will provide insight and make recommendations for program design principles and future research.

An important related question regards how limited resources for subsidies and other incentives should be spent. Yalcintas and Kaya (2009: 3270) makes the point that in Hawaii

---

[15] The 2012 IEPR proceeding, including scope, workshops and presentations, can be found at: http://www.energy.ca.gov/2012_energypolicy/.

[16] CPUC, Opinion Modifying Decision 06-01-024 and Decision 06-08-028 in Response to SB 1, Decision 06-12-033 (December 14, 2006), available at http://docs.cpuc.ca.gov/word_pdf/FINAL_DECISION/63031.pdf

there has been greater legislative effort and more financial incentives to promote renewable energy than energy efficiency. After studying the extent to which energy efficiency is more cost-effective in the commercial sector, they recommend that "it should be a requirement for large-scale buildings, including residential, commercial, and industrial facilities, to retrofit existing inefficient building-equipment with energy efficient technologies before installing PV…" (Yalcintas and Kaya 2009: 3273). Taking the cost-effectiveness comparison in another direction, Mahone et al. (2009) argue that if California increases the Renewable Portfolio Standard to 33%, as recent legislation (SB 2 (1X), 2011) has mandated, then more energy-efficiency investment should also be deemed cost-effective; if not then the case can be made that policy is actively supporting inefficient allocation of resources. Sovacool (2009) generally emphasizes the importance of taking action in all policy areas that affect renewable energy and energy-efficiency adoption, finding that a "comprehensive" policy approach is needed to overcome high barriers of various types (i.e. market, regulatory, cultural, and aesthetic.) Ekins (2004: 1991) cites the need to design "policy packages" that include renewables, efficiency, and nuclear power to achieve the greatest diffusion and meet the ambitious goal of decarbonizing our energy system.

This study is dedicated to examining the electricity consumption behavior of PV households in an effort to understand and improve policy support of small-scale solar adoption. In the aggregate, the study will inform the broader set of policy options available as California moves aggressively towards a lower carbon future. There will be many new opportunities for program integration, and this study seeks to inform the discussion in a way that promotes the types of coordination and integration that will improve program efficiency and deployment impact, and thus result in the greatest carbon savings possible with the available subsidy dollars.

### 1.6. Summary and Roadmap of the Dissertation

This dissertation is organized into six chapters, with this summary and introduction as Chapter 1. Chapter 2 reviews the relevant literatures and sets forth the methodological approach. The primary relevant literatures regard the take-back effect and innovation diffusion. In broad terms, the methodological approach involves the quantitative analysis of a variety of data regarding 5,243 residential solar system installations located in SDG&E service territory, the energy consumption of the electricity customers who purchased them, and the properties at which they were installed.

Chapter 3 characterizes the population of residential PV systems installed under the CSI program, as well as what is known about their adopters. Specifically, it describes the technical and economic characteristics of these systems, analyzes the influence of the electricity rates on the NEM- PV value proposition; and presents the relevant available information regarding the properties where the systems are located.

Chapter 4 focuses on the solar system sizing decision, which is typically the result of a transaction between a residential customer and a solar sales agent such as an installation contractor. It describes the method and results of an analysis designed to characterize consumers' solar system sizing choices given their pre-installation consumption levels and other available information. Systems are ranked according to relevant metrics: percent energy offset, economic optimality, and system cost-effectiveness. With this basis, patterns are deduced and discussed for both customers and their solar contractors.

Chapter 5 is dedicated to analyzing pre- and post-installation consumption data for the subset of 2,410 systems for which at least one year of both pre- and post-installation billing data were available from the utility, and to examining the resulting trends. It first describes the methods utilized to estimate the temperature-corrected energy consumption change between the pre- and post-installation periods. The analysis then determines which households in the sample increased their consumption after solar installation, which decreased consumption and which remained similar, identifying and discussing the trends.

Chapter 6 concludes with a summary of this dissertation's findings and a discussion of its policy implications.

# Chapter 2. LITERATURE AND METHODS

## 2.1. LITERATURE REVIEW

Two sets of literature inform the present study: the energy efficiency literature's discussion of a "take-back" or "rebound" effect; and the innovation diffusion literature. The take-back effect captures the idea that decreasing the marginal cost of energy by making it cheaper and/or more abundant through investment in energy efficiency may encourage increased usage of energy. This dissertation develops the concept of a "solar rebound effect." As with energy efficiency, solar system installation may present occasion for a take-back effect as it may reduce the marginal cost of energy to the consumer

This study links to the innovation diffusion literature by focusing on a set of solar "innovators" to understand more about the conditions under which they change behavior. Much of the innovation diffusion literature has been focused on the processes associated with adoption of a single innovation. In cases like the one under study, a group of potential innovations exists, each of which possesses a signature set of attributes. The research thus expands the innovation literature to accommodate multiple and related innovation adoptions.

### 2.1.1. The Take-Back Effect

This dissertation investigates how residential energy consumption changes with the installation of a solar electric generation system. It is hypothesized that for some households, there may be a "solar take-back" effect akin to the "take-back" or "rebound" effect that has been documented in the energy efficiency literature. This section first explains the energy efficiency take-back effect, and then explains why a similar effect may be present in the context of home-based energy generation.

The take-back effect has been the subject of a sizeable literature, beginning in the 1980s with the work of Khazzoom (1980; 1987). Khazzoom argued that technological improvements that caused efficiency improvements in household appliances would not result in an equal reciprocal reduction in energy consumption. Rather, the efficiency improvements would lead to a reduction in the "price content" of energy in the provision of the final consumer product, and consumers would respond by increasing their energy demand. This increase in demand negates the presumed one-to-one relationship between efficiency improvements and energy savings. "Put simply the rebound effect is the extent of the energy savings produced by an efficiency investment that is taken back by consumers in the form of higher consumption, either in the form of more hours of use or a higher quality of energy service" (Herring and Roy 2007: 195).

The take back effect is most commonly expressed as a percentage. To say that there is a take-back or rebound effect of 10% "means that 10% of the energy efficiency improvement initiated by the technological improvement is offset by increased consumption" (Berkhaut, Muskins et al. 2000: 426). A take-back effect of 10% may also be indicated with the statement that the technological improvement that caused the efficiency gain is 90% effective in reducing energy consumption (cf. Greening, Greene et al. 2000: 394).

In the context of solar self-generation the question is similar: does a decrease in electricity cost to the consumer result in more liberal use of electricity? The installation of a solar system impacts the customer's relationship to the electricity s/he consumes in two ways. First, the system shifts some of the energy supply burden away from the utility—i.e. the kWh consumption paid to the utility decreases. The utility bill decreases, and for most systems the overall transaction decreases the total cost of utility energy for the consumer. Equally, if not more important, the solar system usually reduces the marginal cost of energy directly by offsetting high-tier energy such that the remainder purchased from the utility is at a lower, less expensive tier. This is distinct from energy efficiency: rather than reducing energy consumption for a given service, solar directly reduces the marginal and/or average cost of the energy itself.

The impact on the cost of service for the customer, though, is similar in that the installation of a solar-electric system impacts the customer's total, average and marginal costs of energy. With California's aggressively-tiered electricity rates, under which the marginal cost of energy increases with consumption, the decrease in cost of electricity procured from the utility can be very substantial after solar installation. Solar adoption is thus an interesting case in which to test the idea that post-installation adaptation in the adopters' utility functions results in increased overall electricity consumption.Khazoom's conceptualization of the rebound effect has been labeled in later literature as the "direct rebound effect" (Greening, Greene et al. 2000: 390; Barker, Ekins et al. 2007: 4935-36; Herring and Roy 2007: 196). As Greening et al (2000: 390) note, for consumers the direct rebound effect can be further decomposed into a "substitution" effect and an "income" effect. Substitution means the increased use of the service at hand, i.e. more hours of lighting utilized after a lighting retrofit, while income effects indicate the redistribution of the savings from the lighting measure to other energy end uses, perhaps due to satiation of the need for lighting. As Herring (2007: 195) says: "Many consumers, realizing that the light now costs less to run, are less concerned about switching it off, indeed they may leave it on all night, for example for increased safety or security."

While in the energy efficiency literature it has not been possible to empirically distinguish these two complementary sources of rebound, the difference between them is nonetheless instructive for this study. Since PV systems are not energy consuming devices, such direct substitution cannot occur, so a direct solar take-back would be entirely due to the income effect. That is, consumers facing reduced total and/or marginal cost of electricity due to the installation of a solar system would, in theory, increase overall electricity consumption (presumably prioritizing those end uses with highest marginal utility). Conceiving of the problem in this way has the advantageous result that the unit of analysis is the household and not any particular end use within it, which allows the use of whole-house consumption data rather than disaggregated appliance-level energy usage data. The price we are concerned with is actually the electricity price itself, not the cost per unit of a particular energy service.

Other types of rebound effects include "secondary" (or "indirect") rebound effects, and "economy-wide" rebound effects. The indirect or secondary rebound effect is based on the idea that the overall direct savings from energy efficiency improvements may lead to greater consumption of other products and services beyond the immediately substitutable energy services—i.e. a broad range of goods and services within the household utility function, some of which themselves require energy inputs (Greening, Greene et al. 2000: 391; Sorrell 2007: 41-44). The economy-wide rebound effect extends the direct and indirect rebound effects to the macroeconomic level. It embraces the notion that energy efficiency improvements that lead to lower energy costs will reduce the price of goods and services throughout the economy, which in turn could lead to an increase in energy consumption (see e.g. Greening, Greene et al. 2000; Barker, Ekins et al. 2007).

There is considerable diversity of opinion on the extent and scale of economy-wide rebound effects, with Herring (2007) seeing them as quite important, while Schipper and Grubb (2000) and others (Berkhaut, Muskins et al. 2000) see them as having minimal if any impact. Some studies (Wiser, Bolinger et al. 2005; Ehrhardt-Martinez and Laitner 2008) describe the reduction in natural gas prices resulting from widespread deployment of energy efficiency and renewables as potentially producing the lion's share of their public benefit, outweighing even the direct customer savings from these investments—and they make no mention of any take-back effect at all due to such secondary price reductions. There is general acceptance of the idea that overall utility functions, individual and societal, may change with reduced expenditure on energy.

PV adoption differs conceptually from energy efficiency with respect to its economy-wide effects, given that distributed PV substitutes for utility generation directly rather than as an improvement in the efficiency of a particular group of end uses. PV's reduced energy costs may be primarily project-specific and local such that impacts of widespread adoption may not permeate the economy in the same ways as energy efficiency improvements (cf.Herring and Roy 2007: 197). Certainly massive adoption of distributed PV would have economy-wide impacts with implications for economic development and potentially even structure; however these impacts may not fit within the definition of take-back.

For the purposes of the present study, the direct rebound effect, as identified by Khazoom and elaborated by others, is of greatest interest, both because it is certainly the largest component of the rebound effect and because it is the most quantifiable. The direct rebound effect is essentially due to substitution: a consumer demands more of a given energy service because it becomes cheaper (Schipper and Grubb 2000: 368). The effect of the perceived lower cost on demand is referred to as the price elasticity of demand, which is calculated as the ratio of the percentage change in demand to the percentage change in price. As explained by Herring and Roy (2007: 196), price elasticities "vary by commodity and over time, depending on the ability of consumers to respond to price changes either through changes in behavior, substitution of alternatives or technological change." In theory, the higher the price elasticity of an energy service, the greater the rebound effect (Herring and Roy 2007: 198).

Greening et al. (2000) surveyed extant empirical studies to characterize the presence and size of the direct rebound effect. Most studies had focused on residential fuel demand, particularly space heating and cooling, and personal transportation; many lacked data for key variables or made unrealistic assumptions about consumer behavior (Greening, Greene et al. 2000: 392-93). Evaluating the studies' findings and their limitations, Greening et al. estimated take-back effects of 10-30% for residential space heating; 0-50% for residential space cooling; and 20% to 50% for personal transportation (Greening, Greene et al. 2000: 393-96).

Sorrell et al. (2009) more recently reviewed the literature on the direct rebound effect. Similarly to Greening et al. (2000), the authors observed that the studies diverged in their definitions, methodological approaches and data sources, making assimilation of their findings difficult. Sorrell et al. (2009:1360) observe that the direct rebound effect has been most thoroughly studied in the personal transport sector, and that the effect is likely to lie between 10 and 30% (Sorrell, Dimitropoulos et al. 2009: 1360). For the direct rebound effect in household heating, they find a mean value of 20% (Sorrell, Dimitropoulos et al. 2009: 1362). Small et al (2007) also examine personal transportation, using 2- and 3-stage least-squares models and 35 years of pooled cross-section data, and find relatively small short- and long-run rebound effects: 3% and 10-15%, respectively. The review by Sorrell et al. (2009) is particularly useful for understanding the various methodological options and issues that arise in quantifying the direct rebound effect.

This dissertation builds on and extends the take-back effect literature by conceptualizing a take-back effect associated with residential electricity generation systems and empirically examining its presence and magnitude in the case of residential solar systems. The solar take-back effect investigated herein encompasses the idea that a certain percentage of residential solar generation is taken back by households in the form of higher overall electricity consumption (cf. Herring and Roy 2007: 195). This increase in consumption, if present, would qualify a presumed one-to-one relationship between the amount of solar energy generated and the amount of grid-supplied energy avoided.

In California, installation of a residential solar system is likely to decrease a household's marginal costs of electricity (Darghouth, Barbose et al. 2010).[17] Economic theory suggests, in turn, that such a decrease will increase electricity consumption (cf. Sorrell 2007: 1). As pointed out by Greening et. al.(2000) in the context of energy efficiency, the size of the decrease in the effective price of energy services due to an efficiency improvement depends upon the underlying cost structure. In the case of the solar take back effect, the size of the price decrease due to the use of a solar system will also depend on the underlying cost structure. This cost structure is currently determined by the applicable electricity rates (tariffs); in California, two essential elements of electric rates are their structure and the compensation mechanism for behind-the-meter generation. The former is characterized by increasing block rate structures. The latter defined by net energy metering (NEM, or "net metering"), to which we turn next.

By 2010, almost all states had passed net metering laws that require that utility customers with solar PV systems connected to the grid receive full or partial retail credit for the electricity they generate (Keyes, Fox et al. 2009). Where retail net metering is not available, the utility may only pay the household the wholesale rate for the power (Coughlin and Cory 2009: 5). In this case the marginal incentive for generation would thus be the wholesale price, which is generally much lower than the retail electricity rate charged to households.

States that have net metering laws treat excess generation in various ways. Many net metering laws allow the system owner to get credit for any power generated and consumed for up to a year (Martinot, Wiser et al. 2005). If a system generates more

[17] The post-installation marginal cost of energy depends upon the applicable utility rate structure as applied to the customer's residual energy use. Lower-tier energy is less expensive than higher-tier energy; under NEM, installation of a solar system will tend to push the monthly marginal unit of utility-supplied energy into a lower tier. The PV system itself represents a retrospective sunk cost, and while the method of its purchase will impact the ongoing cost of ownership, this cost is constant and will not vary with subsequent household electricity consumption.

electricity than the household consumes over the year, then the utility may pay the household the wholesale rate or may be allowed to keep the excess power without any payment at all to the system owner (Coughlin and Cory 2009: 5). The latter was the case in the state of California through 2009.[18] In this case, the marginal value of generated electricity will be zero if residential system produces beyond that which it consumes on an annual basis.[19] This creates a strong incentive to size the system not to generate more than will be consumed on site, or if such is already the case, to consume the excess. Where net metering laws require utilities to buy back "excess" generation, the marginal value of electricity for the household up to the amount generated will be the buy-back price, which is typically less than the retail price.

In most cases, however, residential solar systems do not produce more gross energy than the household consumes. Rather, the typical household supplements its self-generation with electricity from the grid. In this situation, the system is still likely to decrease the marginal cost of electricity because of tiered electricity schedules wherein consumers of electricity pay progressively higher rates with increasing consumption. After the installation of a solar system, households will consume less electricity from the grid and thus usually fall into a lower-priced tier. The price of electricity in the lower tier becomes the new, lower marginal cost of electricity. As discussed in Chapter 5 of this study, 96% of the systems for which a full year of both pre- and post-installation utility data were available have a lower marginal cost of utility-purchased electricity during the first year after installation. Further, all PV adopters have a lower average cost of utility energy after PV installation. We investigate there whether post-installation consumption patterns differ for the groups discussed.

The benefits of NEM are substantial; it is essentially a subsidy of $0.88 per Watt of capacity from utility ratepayers as a whole to each installing residential customer. The CPUC's March 2009 NEM Cost-Effectiveness study quantified the overall program levelized cost at $20 million/year as of the end of 2008 (Energy + Environmental Economics 2011). If the CPUC's IOU territories were to meet their overall solar-DG goals of 2,550 MW by 2017, this cost would rise to $137 million /year, roughly 0.4% of the utilities' revenues, and representing a 0.4 cent per kWh price increment for all IOU customers in 2020 (CPUC 2010).

---

[18] AB 920 was signed into law in 2009, for implementation by the Public Utilities Commission in 2010-11. AB 920 requires the utilities to pay compensation to the NEM customer for net excess generation at a rate corresponding roughly to the utility's avoided cost of energy. Details and precise net-energy compensation rates for each utility are being determined by the CPUC within rulemaking R. 10-05-004.

[19] Darghouth et al. (2010: xii) show that for more than 90% of residential customers, bill savings from NEM could be maximized with a system that did not offset 100% of customer load. Optional time-of-use (TOU) rates would be the best choice for customers with larger systems, since PV systems produce relatively more energy during on-peak times, so that on average the offset energy is higher-value than that purchased from the utility. This produces discontinuities for such high-offsetting PV customers, which are important to recognize for customer decision making as well as in the context of AB 920 implementation: namely, a "dead band" of uncompensated production, between the full offset of the customer's bill and its respective full onsite energy consumption.

Whether or not a system generates more than the respective customer's on-site consumption, owners of residential solar systems may be more inclined to use their air conditioning more often or install a hot tub—in part because they generate electricity themselves. Although neglecting to factor in sunk costs is considered to be irrational by economists, studies have shown that many decision makers do this in practice (see e.g. Arkes and Ayton 1999; Arkes and Hutzel 2000). In the case of solar energy systems, the fact that owners have sunk the costs into the system may encourage them to use more electricity so as to feel as if they are getting as much "value" out of it as they can. Moreover, when a household sees its monthly bill decrease from, for example, $200 to $20 post-installation, the household may become less concerned about household energy efficiency or conservation, as suggested by Ito (2011). In California particularly, aggressively tiered rate structures result in large reductions in both the marginal and average costs of energy when solar is installed; basic microeconomics would posit that increased consumption is the natural result. On the other hand, an examination of aggressively tiered residential rate structures in California (including those in place during the period of the present study) found that in practice customer conservation behavior in response to marginal pricing signals is fairly weak, for both customers on standard rates and low-income customers (Borenstein 2008).

Observers of the energy efficiency take-back effect have posited that energy pricing policies can mitigate the effect. Greening et al. (2000: 399) suggest that market instruments such as fuel taxes that raise the per-unit price of energy may be needed in order for energy efficiency policy interventions to achieve their associated energy consumption reduction goals. Sorrell (2007: 93) similarly explains that, to reduce the rebound effect, carbon or energy prices should increase over time to ensure that the absolute cost of equivalent energy services remains relatively constant as the building stock transitions to increased efficiency.

Policy interventions may also be necessary to reduce or prevent any solar take-back effect. For example, carbon or energy pricing systems could be implemented that reduce the extent to which solar households face a lower marginal cost for energy after installation. Certainly for some customers such an approach could undercut a primary rationale for installing solar. Also, large solar systems may lead to a marginal retail cost to the customer of zero in at least some policy environments; thus policies that subsidize or otherwise encourage solar installations should ensure that systems are sized appropriately. Customer education and informational support would make these tradeoffs clearer; or subsidy programs could be designed to ensure that the public or ratepayer do not fund installations that do not meet a predefined private cost-effectiveness test, from the social and/or ratepayer perspectives.

Sorrell (2007: v) states as a "key conclusion" that rebound effects are important and that "[f]ailure to take account of rebound effects could contribute to shortfalls in the achievement of energy and climate policy goals." The same may be true of the solar take-back effect, yet few studies have examined how energy consumption changes after the installation of a solar-PV system. Most directly relevant is the work of Keirstead (2006; 2007), who studied a set of ninety households with PV systems in the United Kingdom. Keirstead (2007) asks whether PV yields a "double-dividend" in the sense that households that install PV systems also become motivated to conserve energy. He found that households reported an estimated 6% reduction in energy use, but was unable to acquire data that might verify these energy savings. Bahaj and James (2007) analyzed consumption data from nine subsidized housing units with solar-PV systems in the UK and found that energy consumption tended to increase over the year after the systems were installed. The authors reported a "proliferation of consumer electronic devices within the properties, notably large screen televisions and computers with 'always-on' broadband connections", but did not show whether this phenomenon in their small sample was independent from the general proliferation of broadband, electronics and video devices (Bahaj and James 2007: 2133). The present study will significantly enhance the literature on the interaction of solar installation and energy consumption, through the analysis of pre- and post-installation consumption data from a comparatively large number of households with solar-PV systems.

### 2.1.2. Other Economic Perspectives

The take-back effect literature is useful for explaining economically-rational post-solar increases in energy consumption, but it has little to say about other, possibly irrational, decisions that are also observed in studies of diffusion, including the present investigation. Indeed, the broader traditional economic literature often frames and analyzes decisions in terms of such a rational-choice model, assuming well-informed and economically objective customers (Newell, Jaffe et al. 1998; Olmstead, Hanemann et al. 2007; Costa and Kahn 2011).

Lutzenhizer has used the term "Physical-Technical-Economic Model," or PTEM, to describe the dominant philosophy underpinning energy-related program design and practice in the U.S. during the last several decades. The PTEM perspective has difficulty appreciating the broader cultural and psychological contexts in which energy decisions are made, and thus has often resulted in programs that underperform. Specifically in the energy efficiency realm, in which California is seen as a clear leader, the PTEM approach has produced programs that fail to detect and address the complex motivational reality of the potential program participant; this has produced a litany of programs that have yielded limited success due to under-engagement with the contextual drivers of the decision making processes that they are trying to influence. Under the PTEM, in short:

> "…the consumer is *necessarily* seen as secondary to devices, as a rational user/manager purposively obtaining *services,* and as someone interested in energy efficiency costs and benefits. This is a paradigmatic imperative of the engineered system interests, the power of proto-economic beliefs in rationality (because the alternative is unimaginable), and the requirements that utility regulators treat energy efficiency programs as accountancy problems. In practical terms, this means that residential energy efficiency policy discourse and supporting analysis must be conducted in a highly coded vocabulary that includes specific terms and concepts to be applied to energy consumers" (Lutzenhiser 2009: 13).

Further, consumers do not have, and usually do not pursue, deep technical-economic knowledge to inform their energy-related purchase decisions; indeed, they typically do not see these decisions as primarily energy-related at all, but rather within a broader context that is socially embedded and relatively complex (Lutzenhiser 2009). It is thus not a surprise that consumers' utility functions for home-related projects with an energy component—likely for energy efficiency measures even more so than for solar—do not emphasize purely energy-related benefits. Recently, economists are applying hedonic models and other tools to detect a variety of drivers and trends in the clean energy marketplace. Notably, a solar system tends to confer a "green consumption" benefit to the purchaser, which has measureable value of 3-6% on the resale price for existing and new homes (Dastrup, Zivin et al. 2010; Hoen, Wiser et al. 2011). Additionally, recent work on peer effects presents convincing evidence that attitude of friends and neighbors can significantly impact the adoption decision. Such peer impacts may be geographical, as illustrated by Bollinger and Gillingham (2011), or network-related, as recounted by some of the lead contractors in the residential solar market (Kennedy 2012).

In practice, residential utility customers have cognitive difficulty understanding electricity pricing signals, since these signals are transmitted through a relatively complex tariff structure and delayed by a month or more from the consumption itself. Ito (2011) showed that, for efficiency adoption and conservation behaviors, consumers respond to changes in average rather than marginal price, and that, in California, this effect is present in inland but not coastal communities. The present study permits a similar examination of customer utility bill response in a different context, that of solar adoption.

Interestingly, a significant percentage of solar households do not undertake energy efficiency improvements that would have been more cost effective and that would have enabled them to install a smaller, more cost-effective solar system (Yalcintas and Kaya 2009: 3269). Conversely, some solar households decrease their energy consumption despite the absence of an additional financial incentive to do so (i.e. even though marginal cost of electricity has decreased as a result of installing solar.)

Adoption of energy efficiency measures by PV customers has been subject to some study within the CSI. The 2010 CSI Impact Evaluation, covering the 2007 to 2009 period, presents results of a survey of 500 program participants and found that more energy efficiency improvements are implemented among CSI participants than a sample group. (Itron 2010) While for self-reported measures the adoption rate is higher among CSI participants, the results are not definitive: adoption of IOU-incentivized efficiency measures similar in both groups, so it is unclear whether some reporting bias is present. The majority of CSI participants surveyed indicated that their solar installer did indeed discuss efficiency opportunities with them, but only a small portion indicate that the contractor presented efficiency in context of sizing the solar system itself, which shows that solar contractors as a group are not fully committed to the energy efficiency proposition. Anecdotal evidence supports this general characterization of solar contractors; while in 2012 more contractors integrate efficiency with solar, these longstanding attitudes generally persist.

The New Solar Homes Partnership (NSHP) program's efficiency requirements have had a greater effect on solar sizing than is evident for the general-market CSI. An analysis of the NSHP program in 2010 notes that the average system size for NSHP is 3.1 kW vs. 4.8 kW in the CSI program, presumably because the homes are designed and built with energy efficiency measures that reduce demand and consequently the required size of the PV system (Itron 2011). The report speculates that "while a number of homes installing PV systems under the CSI GM [general market program] may have employed energy efficiency measures, they had a weaker mandate for energy efficiency; hence, their PV system sizes tended to be larger." Causality is difficult to establish, however, since the earlier analysis described above indicates that the majority of CSI participants did not size their solar system to account for post-energy efficiency improvements, even if they implemented them. Further, there is certainly greater performance variation, and lower average performance, in the existing home stock than in newly constructed homes, such that all else equal one would expect larger system sizes in existing homes. In the actual marketplace, packaging energy efficiency improvements and solar together or in series in strict application of the loading order has proven more difficult for existing than for new homes.

There has been no formal analysis of consumption or peak demand impacts from energy efficiency requirements in the two programs. While this dissertation does not specifically examine the role of efficiency measures within overall trends in post-solar-adoption energy consumption, we can consider adoption of energy efficiency measures as part of a broader idea of behavior change toward (or away from) lower levels of energy consumption.

### 2.1.3. Innovation Diffusion

The literature on innovation diffusion is useful in explaining the non-economic aspects of consumer adoption of clean energy technologies and practices.[20] As a study of households that have installed residential solar systems, this dissertation focuses on "innovators," the earliest adopters of a technological innovation (see Faiers and Neame 2006; Faiers, Neame et al. 2007). The results of data analysis in this dissertation, however, present a puzzle: might households that have proven to be innovators in the area of household energy technologies by installing solar systems not be innovators with respect to taking energy efficiency measures? By exploring the answer to this question, this dissertation contributes new insight into how related energy innovations may be promoted.

Innovation diffusion theory seeks to explain the adoption of innovations among the members of a social system, where innovation is defined as "an idea, practice, or object that is perceived as new by an individual or other unit of adoption" (Rogers 2003: 12). As developed over the past 50 years by Rogers (1962; 1983; 1991; 1995; 2003), the theory consists of several aspects which are often studied independently: (1) the innovation-decision process; (2) adopter categories; (3) communication networks and the role of change agents; and (4) the attributes of an innovation. Scholars of innovation diffusion have often sought to characterize and analyze one or more these theoretical aspects in the context of a given innovation.

The innovation-decision process as elaborated by Rogers consists of five stages through which the innovation adopter moves (Rogers 2003: 168). After gaining initial knowledge of an innovation (knowledge), the adopter forms an attitude about it (persuasion), makes a decision to adopt or reject it (decision), implements it (implementation), and then forms an opinion about whether adoption was the best course of action (confirmation).

---

[20] Note that this should not be read to imply that the innovation diffusion literature is inconsistent with a rational choice perspective, as explained by Faiers et al. (2007: 4386). Innovation diffusion theory not only agrees that much of the buying process is determined by a rational calculus of costs and benefits, but also recognizes that "individuals also utilize their emotional perspective and may choose to either ally or distance themselves to goods or services they like or dislike." As Lutzenhiser (2009) and other social scientists argue, the definition of "rational" implicit in the PTEM encompasses only a small part of the spectrum of what could be reasonably considered rational behavior. The present work aims empirically to untangle some of these questions.

Diffusion of innovation theory views the members of a social system as falling into one of five adopter categories based on consumer personality and behavior, values and attitudes (Rogers 2003: 267; Faiers and Neame 2006: 1798). Adopter categories include innovators (2.5% of adopters); early adopters (12.5%); early majority (35%); late majority (35%); and laggards (15%). Rogers (2003: 273) depicts an S-shaped adopter distribution curve in which the rate of adoption rises slowly as the few venturesome and risk-taking innovators and early adopters take part. The rate of adoption then accelerates as the early majority and late majority come on board. Finally, the rate decreases as the traditionalist laggards slowly adopt the innovation. Rogers's adopter categories have been criticized as lacking empirical support and as being "stereotypical and value-laden terms, which fail to acknowledge the adopter as an actor who interacts purposefully and creatively with a complex innovation" (see also Gatignon and Robertson 1985: 861; Greenhalgh, Robert et al. 2004: 598). The adopter categories have also been found not to be consistent across product categories; in other words, an innovator in one product category is not necessarily an innovator in the next (Gatignon and Robertson 1985: 861; Faiers and Neame 2006: 1799).[21] This is important when contemplating how specific innovations that might at first glance seem comparable may in practice be quite distinct in adoption mechanisms and rates: namely solar and energy efficiency. In our case, for example, income level may correlate very differently with adoption of solar as compared to efficiency measures.

Innovation theory also focuses on communication channels and networks, and the special role of change agents. Rogers emphasizes the importance of interpersonal communication: while mass media may get adopters to the awareness stage, interpersonal communication is often necessary to effect the persuasion that leads to a positive adoption decision (Rogers 2003: 205). An innovation reaches a critical mass of adoption with the emergence of "opinion leaders" who influence other individuals' attitudes and behavior (Rogers 2003: 330, 343). Opinion leaders and others may be influenced by "change agents," who are professionals that represent agencies or organizations with an interest in promoting a particular innovation (Rogers 2003: 27-28). There is some recent evidence that peer effects ("word-of-mouth") strongly influence solar diffusion in California, particularly in communities with lower environmentalist sentiment (Bollinger and Gillingham 2010; Dastrup, Zivin et al. 2010). Another change agent is important to consider in the solar context: the solar industry representative most intimately in contact with the customer him/herself is the sales agent, who is usually—though not always—an employee of the installation contractor itself. This sales approach differs from the energy efficiency supply chain, and we will investigate whether and how much the sales agents and contractors themselves influence the details of the solar adoption decision.

Finally, innovation diffusion theory looks to how innovations are perceived in explaining their differential adoption rates. Innovations are said to have five predominant characteristics or attributes: relative advantage, compatibility, observability, trialability, and complexity. Relative advantage is the degree to which an innovation is perceived as an

---

[21] For studies particularly relating to environmental (green) consumers and the adoption of green innovations, see Laroche (2001), arguing that an adopter of one "green" technology isn't necessarily adopter of all, and Pedersen (2000), stating that "individuals' purchasing behavior is not predictable between eco-products. For example, green consumers will not necessarily favour green energy products."

improvement over the product or practice that it will replace (Rogers 2003: 229). Its "subdimensions" include "economic profitability, low initial cost, a decrease in discomfort, social prestige, a saving of time and effort, and immediacy of reward." Compatibility is a measure of how well the innovation aligns with the values, past experiences and needs of potential adopters (Rogers 2003: 240). Observability is the extent to which the results of an innovation are visible to members of the social system, whereas trialability is the extent to which they can experiment with an innovation before full adoption (Rogers 2003: 258). Complexity measures whether an innovation is perceived as difficult to understand and use (Rogers 2003: 257). Complexity is negatively related to the adoption rate, while the others are positively related (Rogers 2003: 266). Studies have suggested that an innovation's relative advantage, compatibility, and complexity are more consistently important across innovation types in influencing adoption than observability and trialability (Faiers, Cook et al. 2007: 4388; Dearing 2009: 509).

Rogers's approach is well-suited to a study of individual adoption behavior in a single geographic region. Much of Rogers' framework was developed with the individual adopter in mind, and the approach has been considered to be underdeveloped by scholars focused on organizational adoption (Lundblad 2003; Greenhalgh, Robert et al. 2004; Greenhalgh, Robert et al. 2005: 66). Also, over a large geographic area, one would have to closely consider "supply side" factors such as market and other infrastructure characteristics that determine the opportunity to adopt (McEachern and Hanson 2008: 2578). Rogers, in contrast, takes a demand-side approach that largely assumes an opportune infrastructure for adoption and directs attention on the factors that explain individual demand (McEachern and Hanson 2008: 2578). This study follows Rogers in its demand-side approach; the case at hand is a relatively homogeneous geographical area with uniform penetration of solar and energy efficiency supply and installation infrastructure. This approach is well-suited to examination of the possibility that differences in adoption efficiency/conservation and solar may result from their particular characteristics as innovations, and the perceptions of them by adopters.

This dissertation focuses on a hypothesis from the diffusion of innovation literature to explain the observed energy consumption patterns: that some adopters of solar will thereafter become adopters of energy conservation and/or energy efficiency because of new knowledge, information and/or attitudes that become available to them. Perhaps most importantly, education around the solar adoption decision, and the solar installation itself, are likely to furnish the household with information about its energy consumption that was previously very difficult to attain. As explained by Faiers et al. (2006: 1798), "Solar systems can raise a householder's awareness of energy consumption by means of a monitoring facility provided with the installation. This enhanced awareness of energy use could encourage further energy efficiency." After installation of a solar system, households also become generators of energy and would have access to information about the amount of energy they are generating, within guidelines set by the particular program in which the homeowner participated.

Several studies have discussed how new information from energy-use monitoring equipment may affect consumption behavior. Stern (1992: 1227) points out that "households systematically misjudge the amount of energy used in home activities." With well-designed monitoring equipment that gives useful feedback, households do not have to guess or estimate. Hargreaves et al. (2010) found that households that installed "smart meters" all reported some change in their energy use behavior, such as turning devices off when meter readings were high and making plans to purchase more energy efficient appliances. He and Greenberg (2009: 2-3) emphasize that to change household behavior monitoring devices will need not only to provide useful feedback, but also do it in a way that motivates them such as by presenting the information in a vivid and personalized way or making clear the monetary loss that results from energy uses. In his study of households with solar-PV systems, Kierstead (2007: 4135) observed that monitors showing the household's energy generation profile led close to half (43%) of household to engage in some form of load-shifting behavior.

Potential explanations for differences in post-solar-adoption energy consumption may be found in the different perceived attributes of each. With respect to relative advantage, Faiers et al. (2006: 1802-03) show that residential solar is perceived positively in the sense that it reduces pollution, constitutes a safe form of energy generation, generates savings, provides a visual statement of beliefs, and provides reliable and comprehensive energy services. Farhar and Coburn (2000) found similar perceptions of relative advantage in a study of solar adopters in Colorado. In contrast to these positive perceptions, however, solar's relative advantage suffers from negative perceptions of its cost-efficiency, particularly its reputation for prolonged payback period. Energy efficiency improvements might be perceived to have greater cost-effectiveness, but not provide advantages in terms of social prestige or the immediacy of the reward.

Solar is unique from most long-lived purchases made by consumers today—homes, cars etc.—in that it has an infrastructural quality absent from other acquisitions. Customer-based generation that is connected to the public grid displaces energy that heretofore was, and otherwise would be, procured by the monopoly regulated utility, transmitted, delivered and sold to the customer at the meter. Thus the customer's perception of relative advantage is often intertwined with perceptions of their utility, which are widely variable.

A solar system may have a higher degree of compatibility with past experience in the sense that it is a simple replacement of one energy source for another without need for the types of lifestyle or purchasing changes implied by energy conservation and efficiency. Both solar energy and energy efficiency are likely to have high degrees of value compatibility in the case of homeowners that have environmental concerns. Stern (1986: 207) notes that some people have a sense of moral obligation to use energy efficiently. Adachi and Rowlands (2010: 35) find that all participants in their study of residential solar-PV adopters expressed sustainability-related concerns as part of their reason for adopting, and sustainability emerged as the "primary driver" for adoption among identified factors.

Complexity (or conversely simplicity) may be another factor that favors solar. At present in California, the installation of a solar system is a one-step process that is generally contracted out: of the over 6,000 residential PV systems installed in San Diego from 2007 through 2010, only 2.5% were self-installed. Energy efficiency measures tend to consist of a variety of steps, many of which may be considered do-it-yourself projects (Darley and Beniger 1981: 151, 158-59). On the other hand, some potential adopters may perceive solar as complex given its more sophisticated technological nature and the possibility that different solar installers offer various systems which may vary with respect to size and price (Jager 2008: 1937-38). Labay and Kinnear (1981) find that knowledgeable non-adopters, defined as those interested in residential solar heating and hot water systems, who had searched for information about them, perceived solar energy as significantly more complex than those that had adopted the technology. Through consideration of these attributes, this study explores how the motivations for adoption of solar may be different from those of energy efficiency even though both are home energy technologies.

With respect to observability and trialability, solar systems and energy efficiency and conservation measures also differ. Energy efficiency/conservation improvements vary in their trialability, with an improvement like insulation being less trialable, and a conservation measure like turning down the thermostat being more trialable (Darley and Beniger 1981: 158). A solar system, however, is likely to be perceived as less trialable than most efficiency and conservation measures. Observability, on the other hand, can be expected to favor solar systems as they tend to be more visible to the community (Bollinger and Gillingham 2010). A survey of residential solar PV owners in San Diego found that neighbors often ask about their systems (City of San Diego and California Center for Sustainable Energy (CCSE) 2009: 4).

### 2.2. Research Methods

This section describes the broad methodology of the study and the various data sources that are used, addressing issues of data reliability and completeness. More detailed discussions of the methods used to complete the analyses of Chapters 3, 4 and 5 are included in those chapters.

#### 2.2.1. Data Summary

The primary approach used in this study is quantitative analysis of two large data sets. The CPUC and SDG&E granted the author access to these customer data. The CPUC also approved provision of similar data to the author from PG&E and SCE, which could be used in the future for an analysis with statewide coverage.

The first data set includes information about the characteristics of all residential solar-PV installations under the California Solar Initiative program in the SDG&E service territory, which includes San Diego County and southern Orange County. 6,132 residential solar-PV systems were installed between the program's initiation in January 2007 and December 31, 2010. Fields include the physical addresses of all installed systems; date of installation; system component details, installation characteristics such as module tilt, array azimuth and other derate factors such as shading; installing contractor; system seller (which may be different from the installer); system owner; system costs; program incentive amount; and many other details related to the application process, and program process information. The author has unique and intimate understanding of the CSI program itself and this database specifically through his professional employment at the California Center for Sustainable Energy, which administers the CSI program in SDG&E service territory.

The second large data set contains monthly electricity consumption data for the more than 6,000 CSI participant residences whose systems were installed between January 1, 2007 and December 31, 2010. SDG&E electric billing data for the period between January 2006 and December 2010 were provided to the author by SDG&E. This dataset contains the monthly net electric consumption, meter read date, applicable electric rate, account number, electric account initiation date (which also serves as a proxy for home purchase date), meter number and utility climate zone for each customer. Additionally, these data include a simple six-bin categorization of the economic status of each of these customers, which SDG&E purchases periodically from a third party for segmentation, outreach and marketing purposes. The data include at least one month of pre-installation and post-installation electricity consumption data for each customer.

### 2.2.2. Supplemental Data Sources

A variety of supplemental data sources also inform the analysis:

a) *Applicable SDG&E residential electric rates for January 2006-December 2010.* As a necessary complement to the monthly consumption data, the rate history for the Domestic Residential (DR) rate was collected from SDG&E. The total rate consists of three separate rate components: the Electric Energy Commodity Charge (EECC); the Utility Distribution Charge (UDC); and the DWR Bond Charge (AB1X). Each component is considered separately and then combined to determine each month's charges. Knowledge of applicable electricity rates is critical for understanding and harvesting the potential economic benefits of net-metered solar. Applying the applicable rate to each month's data for each customer gives us the marginal, total and average cost of utility energy for that customer across the study period.

b) *Comprehensive parcel data from the County of San Diego Assessor.* The most relevant information contained, and the number of properties in our dataset for which data were available is shown in the Table 2.1.

**Table 2.1. Assessor Data Fields**

| Data Field | Number of Parcels |
|---|---|
| Build Year | 3,557 |
| Beds | 3,533 |
| Baths | 3,535 |
| Owner Occupied | 3,181 |
| Living Area | 3,552 |
| Assessed Value | 3,604 |
| Pool | 3,382 |
| Acreage | 1,048 |
| Addition | 1,165 |
| Connected Garage | 3,150 |
| # Garage Stalls | 3,477 |
| Carport | 2,830 |
| Park View | 2,885 |

c) *Territory-wide aggregate residential demand load profiles for 2006-2010.* 15-minute interval data obtained from SDG&E's load research department allows comparison of the study group's monthly electric consumption evolution to overall seasonal and yearly trends for residential customers as a whole.

d) *PBI metered data.*
Through 2010, 115 residential solar customers in SDG&E territory had chosen to receive PBI rather than a one-time up-front EPBB incentive. These residences have dedicated meters that record monthly energy production from the PV system, with which the program administrator calculates each month's incentive payment for the duration of the 60-month PBI period. These monthly production data were compared to SAM/PVWatts modeled production for the 59 residential systems with at least 12 months of post-installation PBI data. The difference between actual and modeled for these 59 PBI systems was then used to calibrate the production model for all systems studied.

*e) Climate zone information.*
Climate zone (CZ) determines the details of rates for residential customers (specifically the baseline allocation) and is thus important to understand the economic impact of each system studied. Further, seasonal energy consumption patterns are directly influenced by the characteristics of the specific CZ in which a property is located. In the study area there are four CZs: Coastal, Inland, Desert and Mountain. Addresses were mapped in ArcView and overlaid with the Utility Climate Zone boundaries to determine the applicable CZ for each installation; this information was confirmed with SDG&E Climate Zone assignment data.

*f) Cooling-Degree Days.*
Monthly actual cooling-degree-days (CDD) and "typical meteorological year" (TMY) were obtained from the National Weather Service for 25 stations throughout Southern CA, covering from January 2006 to September 2010. This information was included in the analysis to control for weather variation, allowing weather-normalized comparisons of energy consumption through time. The data were not complete, with some stations displaying gaps of up to 6 months. The least complete stations were discarded, and other gaps were filled with same-month data from similar nearby stations. To ensure adequate geographical coverage throughout SDG&E territory, a technique called "kriging" was utilized. The kriging process uses the available CDD data for all stations to generate a comprehensive GIS raster set for the territory in question. CDD information from the raster set was then assigned to the specific location for each solar system in the study group.

*g) Electric-only Customers.*
Residential customers without natural gas service have a different, higher baseline allocation than those with both gas and electric service. This information was utilized to ensure accurate determination of utility-based energy marginal, average and total costs for all customers in the study group.

*h) PRIZM Customer Segments.*
SDG&E supplied one of six segment descriptions for each customer, based on commercial data purchased periodically by the utility (see Table 2.2).

**Table 2.2. Socio-Economic Segments used by SDG&E**

| Segment Name | Description |
|---|---|
| Successful | Wealthiest segments of each age group: business executives and senior professionals; acquisitive; range from young high-income families to empty-nesters; disposable income; large homes on large lots |
| Comfortable | Stable, affluent professionals and white-collar workers. Small families and empty-nesters. Suburban homeowners. |
| Established | Mid-career to retired suburban and exurban families, blue-collar workers with some disposable income, high proportion of veterans; moderate-priced housing |
| Professional | Young and middle-aged singles and couples on the urban fringe; dual-income, no children; tech-savvy; white-collar workers |
| Challenged | Blue-collar families living in the suburbs (inland areas of San Diego) |
| Young Mobile | Diverse (many foreign-born and multi-lingual), politically liberal, college-educated urban dwellers, singles and couples. |

Each aggregate segment represents a collection of more specific socio-economic groups described in detail by Nielsen.[22]

### 2.2.3. Data Processing

The two primary datasets, CSI system information and SDG&E billing data, required considerable manipulation in order to be useful for analysis. Here we describe the processes by which these primary data were related, combined, cleaned and filtered.

The CSI database is the most comprehensive solar program database ever developed; in support of much of its information is in fact public.[23] However, fields that might enable identification of individual customers are not included in the public datasets. These fields include customer name, address, account number, meter number. The CPUC granted the author permission to utilize the full dataset for the SDG&E territory for purposes of this research.

SDG&E provided billing data for all of the 6,300+ residential NEM customers installed in its territory after January 1, 2007 and through December 2010. Customer name

---

[22] For full cluster descriptions, see $PRIZM_{NE}$: The New Evolution Segment Snapshots (2003), available at http://www.tetrad.com/pub/prices/PRIZMNE_Clusters.pdf

[23] The CSI public database can be found at Go Solar California, Download Current CSI Data, http://www.californiasolarstatistics.ca.gov/current_data_files/.

of record, service address, account and meter numbers, and other account-specific information was included for each system.

There was no common identifier across the two main datasets, so the first task was to create one. Using a series of matching functions across similar fields in the two datasets, matching was possible with a high degree of confidence for 5,243 systems—that is, where multiple field matches were encountered across name, account number, meter number, address, and/or a visual aerial confirmation using Google Maps. This was a tedious process and uncovered many dozens of errors in the CSI and/or utility databases, most commonly slight differences in name (spouse or partner on one or the other account), address (abbreviations, spacing, concatenation etc.), incorrectly entered account and meter numbers in the CSI database, or similar differences.

Some attrition is expected since not all of these systems received CSI incentives, particularly in 2007 as many residential solar installations had reserved incentives under the ERP program prior to the end of 2006. There are however other reasons for unmatched systems. The CSI database contains information entered by homeowners, contractors and program staff, each of whom may make errors or not understand the importance of completely and accurately entering all of the (literally hundreds) of required data fields. Data quality has improved steadily since the CSI began, but there are still some empty fields and other inaccuracies, particularly for systems installed earlier in the program. In the end, roughly 700 CSI-funded systems were not matchable to utility billing data, primarily not only due to unresolvable differences in customer fields across the two datasets, but also likely due to post-PV-installation changes to account information (home sale or change in occupancy, for example). Given the fact that the customer information in each database was independently created, the matching percentage of over 85% is more than satisfactory. Once matching was completed, the CSI-assigned system number was utilized as the common identifier for the 5,243 system in each dataset, and the two were combined.

Next, the combined dataset was cleaned and filtered. The following systems were excluded:

- Accounts with data gaps during the 12 months prior to PV installation. Accounts with more than two continuous months of very low consumption (less than 100 kWh/month) during the pre-installation period. Such a pattern is not explainable by irregularities in meter reading or billing, and would most likely indicate extended absence or the presence of an existing self-generation system.

- 110 accounts had at least one month of negative consumption. These sites clearly had a previously-installed PV or other self-generation system, which renders difficult understanding of their actual total pre and post energy consumption around the system in question.

    - Accounts on non-standard rates. The main residential rate is the "domestic residential" (DR) tariff; over 95% of CSI participants utilize the DR tariff. Customers on non-DR rates, such as time-of-use (DRTOU) and low-income (DRLI), as well as CARE-qualified customers (California Alternate Rates for Energy), were excluded from the main analysis. Participation of low-income (DRLI and CARE) customers in the mainstream CSI (as opposed to the SASH program) is low, so that that in any case the sample sizes did not allow for robust independent analysis. Low-income customers are a potential target for follow-on analysis, for example to examine income-related variations of the results obtained here. Solar adopters who are on the DRTOU (time-of-use) rate would also be of interest given the coming shift across the state to TOU and real-time pricing being embraced by the CPUC and CEC and enabled by smart meters.

- Accounts without established billing history. Finally, we limited the Chapter 3 group to customers with more than 12 months of pre-installation billing data. The impact was to exclude several hundred accounts that likely adopted solar upon moving into their newly purchased home. Since we are examining changes in consumption due to solar adoption, these accounts are not useful to the analysis.

The result was that 4,355 systems of the originally matched 5,243 systems contain quality system information and have 12 months of credible pre-installation billing data.

### 2.2.4. Methodology

Once the datasets were assembled and cleaned, the author conducted three major steps. The first step was to characterize the installed systems (see Chapter 3). The second step was to analyze how each solar system in the sample was sized with respect to pre-installation electricity consumption and other available information (see Chapter 4). The third step was to model post-installation PV production for all systems, adding this to the remaining utility billed consumption, in order to determine aggregate changes in consumption from the pre- to post-installation periods (see Chapter 5). Detailed descriptions of the methods used in each of these steps are provided in each respective chapter.

The most critical fields are:

- Installation date. SDG&E NEM system billing data contained an "approved on" date field, which refers to approval of the interconnection agreement submitted by the customer (usually by the installations contractor on behalf of the customer). In practice, SDG&E usually performs the actual interconnection within one week of this approval, making it possible to rely on the approval date as a fair proxy for interconnection itself, and better than any field in the CSI database. By excluding one month before and after the approval date, we assure clean pre and post periods for each installation.

Our analysis consisted of the following steps:

- Match and combine with property assessment data. This was a process similar to that utilized for matching the CSI system information and SDG&E billing data; however alignment between the SDG&E and County property data was considerably better, facilitating this merging.

- Incorporate Climate Zone, Electric-only customer fields; identify leased system and generate a field to capture that for each system.

- Model expected PV production for the sizing decision, utilizing typical meteorological year (TMY) solar radiation data. The goal here is to estimate generic output data of the sort that would have been available to the installer and customer during the purchase decision. Thus TMY data are most appropriate here, since they are what the contractor's model would have used.

  NREL's System Advisor Model (SAM) is the optimal tool both for PV production analysis. Utilizing best-practice industry standard algorithms, SAM can provide monthly production estimates based on either TMY or actual solar radiation data, and thus serves the needs of both the pre-installation sizing assessment (using TMY data) and the post-installation production modeling (using actual solar radiation data, though this data must be acquired from a third party). SAM also allows batching routines to be set up via its embedded programming language, which standardizes and speeds the modeling and was essential for efficient processing of the 5,243 systems in our study.

- Characterize the sizing decision for each household with solar, including an analysis of the utility billing impact expected at the moment of installation. Determine *prima facie* which systems in the dataset are sized economically optimally, "oversized" and "undersized." The result is two unique metrics for each system: first, the anticipated percent of pre-installation load to be offset by the PV system; and second, the "sizing index," which expresses the proximity of the anticipated post-installation utility consumption to the customer's respective cost-effectiveness threshold (i.e. 130%-of-baseline). This analysis is the subject of Chapter 4.

- For each customer, utilizing the climate zone and appropriate baseline allocation and applicable electric rate, calculate monthly costs of energy purchased from the utility: total, average and marginal costs. This was done for all available utility data, pre- and post-installation.

- Examine patterns for system sizing and cost, based on installer, pre-installation consumption and cost, customer segment, climate zone, home age and size, etc. The goal is to detect patterns and trends in system sizing. This is also part of the Chapter 4 analysis.

- Obtain <u>actual</u> solar radiation and other necessary weather data across the region, from the SolarAnywhere database. Model each system's expected monthly PV output, again utilizing SAM/PVWatts over its post-installation period (from installation through December 2010).

- Identify system with amorphous modules and generate a field to capture it (important for degradation modeling).

- Model AC-DC derate adjustments and time-dependent degradation factors in the multi-year PV output analysis. The two factors included are a linear monthly degradation factor, and an exponential "initial burn-in" factor (higher for amorphous (a-Si) systems, lower for crystalline systems).

- Calibrate the multi-year PV output estimates using actual PBI metered data from the 59 CSI systems for which it is available. Determine the proper AC-DC derate adjustments, degradation rate and burn-in factors. Adjust the modeled PV outputs for the overall study group with these results.

- For the entire study group, add modeled output to net utility consumption to obtain "modeled total" electricity consumption for each month in the post-installation period.

- Perform pre-post analysis, in two stages (Chapter 5). First, annual aggregated system information was utilized to detect gross trends, determine which households increased consumption and which decreased consumption, and answer in preliminary form the question of whether a solar take-back effect may indeed exist.

- For each system, generate monthly cooling degree days (CDD) from National Weather Service measurements for a group of stations within SDG&E service territory. The three closest National Oceanographic and Atmospheric Administration (NOAA) sites to each PV installation are determined utilizing spatial analysis tools, overlaying the NOAA stations onto a map of the study group installations. The CDD numbers are calculated for each system using distance-based weightings, through a process called kirging. With monthly CDD for each system in hand, we can separate weather effects from other sources of post-installation changes in consumption.

- Seek explanations and suggest policies for increasing the number of systems that are optimally sized, encouraging integration of efficiency measures with solar, and for reducing the solar take back effect. A summary of the analysis and policy recommendations are presented in Chapter 6.

## 2.3. Conclusion

This chapter has reviewed key works from relevant literatures on the take-back effect and innovation diffusion. Questions of technology change and its impacts are central issues for navigating California's movement toward a clean energy future. Scaling up installation of distributed energy resources (DER) is one of the central mechanisms defined in California's policy suite for achieving this transition. Policies that promote DER should reflect an understanding of consumer response to these technologies; however, behavior is still a poorly understood factor within this arena. Both the specific issue of take-back and the broader area of innovation adoption are central to understanding the issue at hand.

This chapter has also set forth ley information regarding research methods. The author has assembled a set of data that allows unique and subtle understanding of the way residential electricity users respond to having a rooftop solar system. There is a robust small-scale solar marketplace in California, one which embeds interesting dynamics at the level of the individual transaction. Our goal in this project is to uncover generalizable trends that can inform policy regarding the best ways to harness and appropriately support the PV marketplace for continued, responsible growth.

In sum, this dissertation is asking a new question with policy relevance, building on existing literatures to frame the potential outcomes. The necessary data were gathered, and the path set for finding an answer for the first time.

# Chapter 3. SOLAR ADOPTION IN THE SAN DIEGO REGION

## 3.1. INTRODUCTION

This chapter will first analyze the solar "value proposition" for solar adopters in the San Diego region. Since virtually all small-scale solar systems (and all the systems in our study group) are connected on the customer side of the meter and subject to net energy metering, understanding NEM is central to understanding the value of solar. And under NEM, electric rates determine the value of energy generated and thus the feasibility of each solar installation. We therefore utilize the primary domestic residential rate used by SDG&E to compare the costs of solar generation to that of energy purchased from the utility.

We then utilize our various datasets, now integrated, to characterize the population of residential solar systems in the San Diego region that were installed between 2007 and 2010, including their capacity, cost, geography, details of the housing stock and basic characteristics of the adopters themselves.

## 3.2. THE VALUE OF SOLAR

The economic value of solar for the customer depends mainly on two elements: the utility bill (and the savings to it subsequent to installing solar generation); and the cost of the solar system itself, whether purchased, financed or leased. The monthly bill is the main communication between the electricity customer and the utility. The cost of the solar system depends on the particulars of the purchase, including the price from the contractor and terms of the sale or lease. Both sides of the equation are fundamental components of the decision to go solar, and they are examined here in turn.

### 3.2.1. SDG&E Residential Electric Rates and Their Evolution

Residential customers have several rate options with the utility. In practice, most residential electricity customers, over 90%, are on the standard domestic residential (DR) rate, with most of the remaining customers on the low-income (DRLI) rate. The DRLI rate is reserved for customers with stated income lower than four times the poverty level. As might be expected for the population of solar adopters, the vast majority are on the DR rate, with only a small portion on other rates including the DRLI. There are also two other rates that are relevant here. First, the DRSES was introduced in the mid-2000s and targeted residential customers with solar energy systems (hence the "SES"). The rate is still open but has not had heavy uptake. Second, the DRTOU is SDG&E's residential time of use rate, under which on-peak energy is more expensive than off-peak, reflecting actual costs of service better than a strictly volume-based tiered rate. California is moving towards using real-time pricing more comprehensively including in the residential sector, so the DRTOU is certainly a precursor of things to come. Finally, the DM rate is applicable to master-metered multifamily facilities, and in 1978 was closed to new customers; only a few residual customers remain on DM.

For the entire group of adopters with both CSI and SDG&E billing information is available, the percentages of participants on each available rate are shown in Table 3.1. However, we focus only on customers utilizing the standard DR tariff, in order to maintain cleanliness for determining trends for mainstream solar adopters in the marketplace today with. As the solar market expands by reducing prices and developing offerings more accessible to lower-income customers, interesting analysis will be possible to determine behavior patterns across a broader spectrum of rates and incomes.

**Table 3.1. Solar Adopter Electric Rates**

| Rate | Number | Percentage |
|---|---|---|
| DR | 4,989 | 95.2% |
| DRLI | 129 | 2.4% |
| DRSES | 69 | 1.3% |
| DRTOU | 41 | 0.8% |
| DM | 15 | 0.3% |
| TOTAL | 5,243 | 100.0% |

In California and other parts of the country, increasing block rate structures (also called "tiered rates") are common. Indeed, since 2001 California's investor-owned utilities have had aggressively tiered rates. As part of the resolution of California's electricity crisis of 2000-2001, AB 1X (2001) imposed a rate cap of around 12 cents per kWh on residential electric consumption up to 130% of the applicable baseline allocation for each customer. This level of consumption corresponds to Tier 1 (baseline) and Tier 2 (100%-130% of baseline). As a result, all residential rate increases since 2002 have been loaded into the upper tiers of consumption, giving rise to a significant jump in the per-kWh charge at the Tier 2-3 threshold. Since the early 2000s in SDG&E territory, the cost of higher-tier energy (Tiers 3 and above) has increased roughly twofold. This high-cost energy has created a clear business opportunity for the residential solar industry, since a small rooftop solar system can produce electricity at a cost well below the cost of upper-tier energy from the utility.

Application of the DR rate varies between customer groups. While the cost per kWh for each respective tier is the same for every covered customer, the baseline allocation varies according to two factors: the climate zone in which the property is located, and whether the home has natural gas service as well as electric. SDG&E territory contains four climate zones, while around 90% of SDG&E customers have both electric and natural gas service. Table 3.2 shows the baseline allocations and tier definitions for the four climate zones, and for standard (gas & electric) and electric-only customers. Allocations do change slightly over time, and this analysis utilizes the applicable ones for each month; the information presented below is representative, and is from 2008.

**Table 3.2. SDG&E Residential Baseline Allowances by Zone and Season**

| Baseline Allowance (kWh/day) | | | | | | Monthly Tiers (consumption blocks) |
|---|---|---|---|---|---|---|
| | Climate Zone | Coastal | Inland | Desert | Mountain | |
| | Zone no. | 1 | 2 | 3 | 4 | Tier 1 = Baseline |
| Basic (G&E) | Summer | 9.6 | 11.2 | 16.4 | 14.8 | Tier 2 = 101-130% baseline |
| | Winter | 10.1 | 10.8 | 11.2 | 13.8 | Tier 3 = 131%-200% baseline |
| All-Electric | Summer | 9.8 | 11 | 19.5 | 17.3 | Tier 4 = 200% baseline and above |
| | Winter | 16.6 | 18.3 | 22 | 28.5 | Tier 5 = 300% and above (prior to 05/08) |

*Source: SDG&E rate sheets, baseline amounts applicable 1/1/2010*

Typical SDG&E domestic residential (DR) electric rates are shown graphically in Figure 3.1; the summer and winter rates correspond to July 2007 and December 2007, respectively. The critical price jump occurs between Tiers 2 and 3: in summer, at the T2-3 threshold, the cost of energy from the utility jumps from around 15 cents to 25 cents. The detailed cost for each tier varies slightly with each rate update filed by SDG&E to the CPUC, but the basic structure has remained the same. This analysis utilizes the actual applicable monthly rates throughout.

**Figure 3.1. Typical SDG&E domestic residential (DR) electric rates**

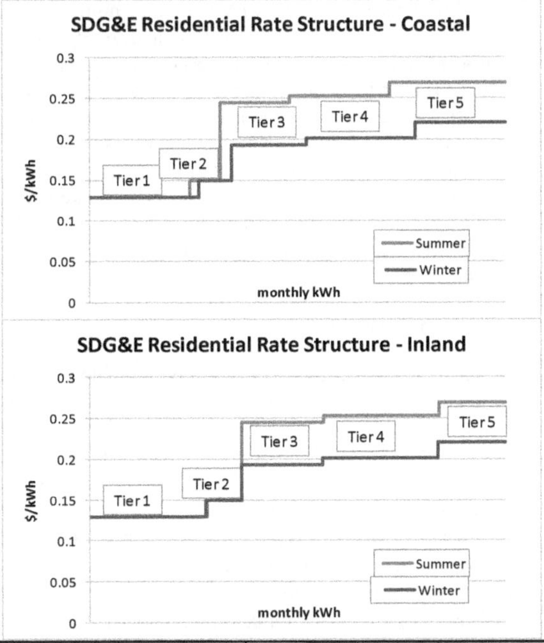


| Tier | Energy Charge ($/kWh) | | Consumption Threshold (kWh/month) Coastal | | Inland | |
|---|---|---|---|---|---|---|
| | Summer | Winter | Summer | Winter | Summer | Winter |
| Baseline | 0.1287 | 0.1287 | 288 | 313 | 336 | 335 |
| Tier 2 | 0.1488 | 0.1488 | 374 | 407 | 437 | 435 |
| Tier 3 | 0.2441 | 0.1927 | 576 | 626 | 672 | 670 |
| Tier 4 | 0.2531 | 0.2015 | 864 | 939 | 1008 | 1004 |
| Tier 5 | 0.2690 | 0.2196 | add'l | add'l | add'l | add'l |

**Summer = June 2007; Winter = December 2007**

*Source: Calculated from the applicable SDG&E tariff sheets.*

The operative point is that this tiered structure creates a clear break point above which the marginal energy cost is well above the expected levelized cost of energy (LCOE) for PV-based electricity that is generated behind the meter. A PV system sized to offset, via NEM, this "upper-tier" energy consumption will be clearly cost-effective. Darghouth et al. (2010) characterized this phenomenon for SCE and PG&E residential customers, and even though the particulars of the rate structures vary somewhat between utilities, the situation is similar for SDG&E customers. Solar vendors understand at least the basics of electric rates, and many of them explicitly "sell to the baseline", meaning that they endeavor to size systems to offset the expensive energy, leaving the baseline and Tier 2 energy to be purchased from the utility. Based on the applicable residential rates, this is a solid business practice.

Typical residential customers, however, do not necessarily understand their electricity bills, even if early adopters of PV tend to be among the more inquisitive of electricity customers. Thus, despite the clearly solar-friendly residential rate structures present in the IOU territories, the adoption decision process is often not made with full information. Ito (2011) utilized SCE and SDG&E rates in his assessment of price as a driver of electricity consumption, and concluded that average (rather than marginal) costs drive behavior. Borenstein (2009) asserts that customers likely act with "constrained optimization" subject to "implementation error," for example due to the fact that they do not fully understand how they are charged for electricity, and likely do not even know when each billing cycle begins. Here, we calculate the average, marginal, and total utility costs for each solar adopter for each month through the study period, in order to analyze practical outcomes for solar adopters.

### 3.2.2. Cost of Solar Generation

A theoretical economically rational, knowledgeable consumer would compare the cost of the energy to be offset from the utility to the cost of generation s/he will incur through investment in a solar generation systems. The LCOE for each system is calculated based on the information known for that system, with the following assumptions:

- System lifetime: 25 years
- Discount rate on future costs (inverter replacement): 7%
- Module degradation: 0.7% per year
- Cash purchase (no financing costs)
- System production: modeled with NREL's System Advisor Model

LCOE is calculated on the total installed cost; second, subtracting the CSI incentive; and third, subtracting both the CSI incentive and the full federal investment tax credit (ITC). The residential ITC was capped at $2,000 until January 1, 2009, at which point it became the full 30% of the installed cost, equivalent to the preexisting commercial ITC. Not all adopters will be eligible for the full ITC, but as a general rule the current adopter population will capture much or all of it. In the background of the figure, the current cost of energy in each tier of consumption (using the predominant "DR" rate) is shown (note that Tier 5 disappeared in May 2008). The figure shows that typical net LCOE is very clearly within or just below Tier 3 electricity from the utility, demonstrating that the typical customer would maximize value with a solar system sized to offset energy from the top tiers, particularly after January 1, 2009. The joint impact of rising top-tier utility price and the increased tax credit seems evident in Figure 3.2: residential solar adoption increased notably more rapidly beginning in January 2009. The installed cost of solar PV systems has declined by 20% since early 2008 as well, such that by the end of 2010 the top-tier cost of energy from the utility was around double the LCOE to the customer who adopts PV and generates that energy himself.

**Figure 3.2. Levelized Cost of Energy Trend**

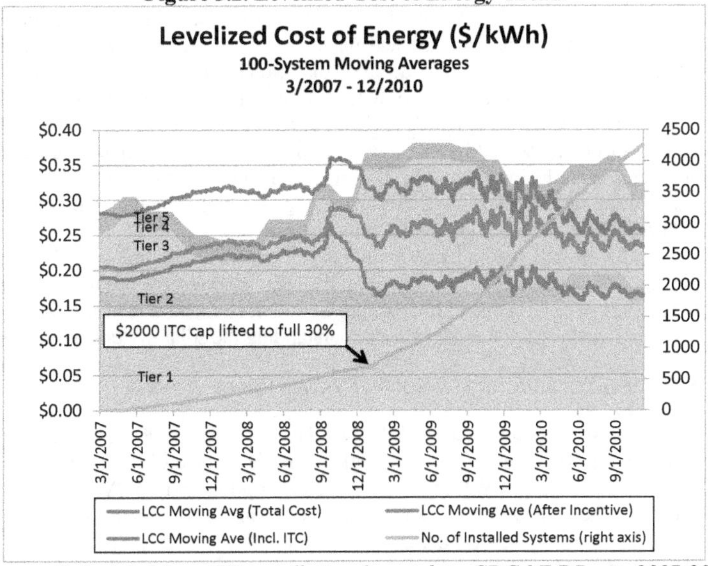


*Source: Calculated from CSI installation & cost data; SDG&E DR rate 2007-2010*

The higher ITC and rising marginal electric rates have more than offset the decline in CSI incentives, thus stimulating the solar market. At the end of 2010, the net benefit of solar for an SDG&E customer consuming energy from tier 4 was clear and large. The marginal kWh of utility energy cost $0.32, while the net LCOE for solar self-generation was $0.16, for a net benefit of $0.16 for each kWh offset by solar, for a customer with creditable tax liability. If the ITC were eliminated, solar LCOE would increase by up to 9 cents/kWh, to 25 cents. Even so, if NEM were to persist in its current form there would still be ample value to the customer from solar adoption. However, if NEM is also reformed or its benefits otherwise diluted, there would be significant downward price pressure on the residential solar marketplace.

In the absence of CSI incentives and the lower ITC, some of the difference could be made up by monetizing the RECs produced by each residential system. Each $10 increment in the REC price corresponds to a $0.01 per kWh benefit to the customer (assuming an automated process with no additional aggregator charge). In order to make up 5 cent per kWh—enough to impact the solar value proposition—RECs would need to be priced at a minimum of $50. That is, the $50 per REC, all going to the customer, would provide 5 cents/kWh toward the customer improve the economic case for solar. At this price, an owner of a 5kW PV system would collect about $450 annually for her RECs. Indeed, $50 is the REC price cap imposed by the CPUC and confirmed by the legislature.[24] However, a $50 price is far higher than the typical current REC price, which in California has generally remained below $10.

Finally, in late 2010, third-party ownership of residential solar was growing very strongly, and by June 2012 represented almost 75% of the residential market. These leasing and power-purchase agreements (PPAs) can provide solar for little or no up-front cost to the customer. At the same time, the leasing and PPA contracts can be complex for the customer to understand. They often include an escalator on the future utility energy price, which presumes that future offset energy will be more expensive and improve the potential solar adopter's perceived value in comparison. However, this escalator may not reflect long-term trends, for two reasons. First, if natural gas pieces remain low, marginal energy costs may not increase per historical trends. Second, if NEM is indeed reformed, the likely result is that that top-tier rates would decrease, leaving essentially "underwater" many solar adopters who based their decision on purely financial criteria.

As the CSI participant population grew strongly beginning in 2009 coincident with the higher federal investment tax credit, the solar marketplace became more dynamic, with a wide range of contractors participating. Contractor-related trends are discussed further in Chapter 4, as they are important for understanding the solar system sizing decision.

## 3.3. Characterizing the Solar System Population

This section characterizes the population of solar system adopters in the San Diego region included in this study. The original dataset included 5,243 installed systems. Systems with any negative values for monthly net consumption prior to PV installation were excluded; these sites clearly already had an existing NEM system. Addresses lacking at least 12 months of pre-installation consumption data were excluded as well. The dataset thus pared contains 4,355 installations.

### 3.3.1. Summary Information

Systems are located primarily in the coastal and inland climate zones, with very few systems located in the Mountain and Desert zones (see Figures 3.3 and 3.4). This distribution reflects the location of the region's population broadly. At the same time, the market is still small in absolute terms, with less than 2% adoption among single-family residential customers, and shows considerable geographic clustering at the neighborhood level.

[24] The $50 REC price cap was established by the CPUC in March 2010 in Decision 114750, extended by the CPUC in January 2011 in D.441596, and maintained by SBX1-2 (Simitian), signed by the Governor in April 2011.

**Figure 3.3. SDG&E Climate Zones**

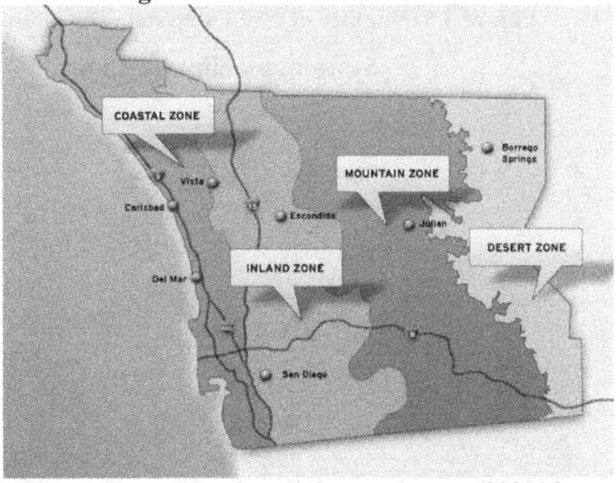


*Source: SDG&E, Climate Zones Map, http://sdge.com/images/3335/climate-zones-map.*

Our dataset reflects the general distribution of PV system in the region. Figure 3.5 shows the number of systems in each climate zone, along with the average size system in each. As the solar market has grown and matured, and as prices have dropped, a slow but noticeable inland installation trend inland has emerged. The value of offsetting summertime top-tier utility energy is certainly one of the factors driving this trend.

**Figure 3.4. CSI Residential Solar Capacity by Zip, SDG&E Territory, 2006-2010**

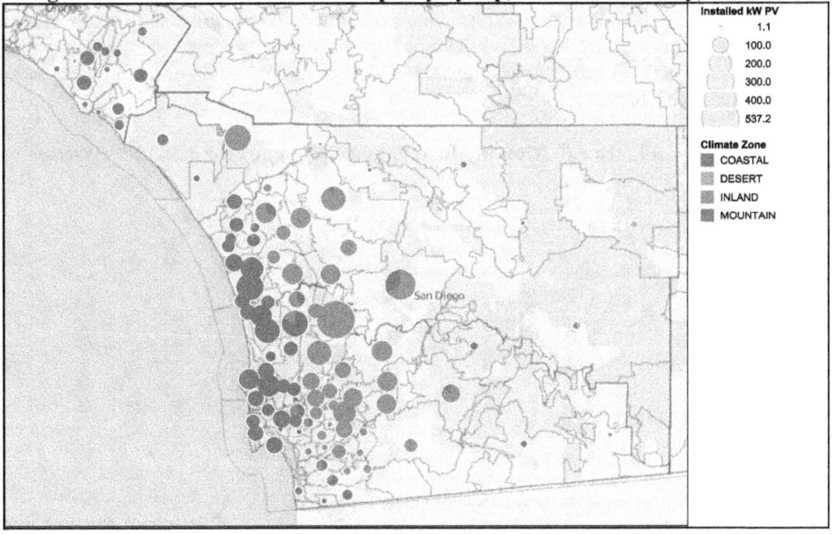

*Source: Constructed by author using CSI data.*

**Figure 3.5. Number of CSI PV Systems by Climate Zone**

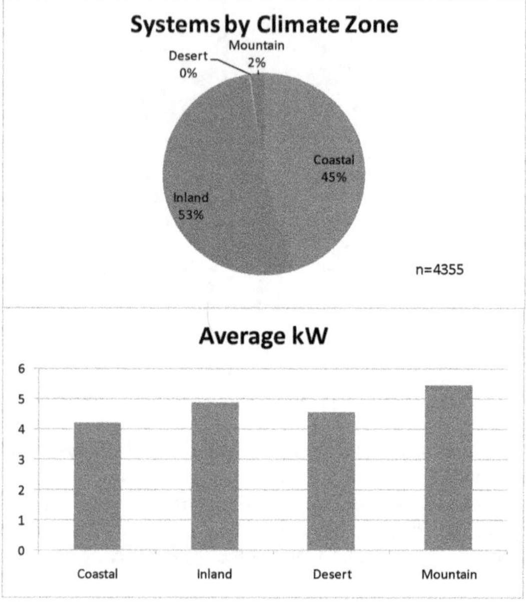


Installation activity is occurring year-round, though fall is the season with greatest project flow. Figure 3.6 shows the monthly installation frequency for our study group; installations peak in October. This may assist our interpretation of the pre/post energy analysis in Chapter 5.

**Figure 3.6: Monthly Installation Frequency for 4,355 PV Systems**

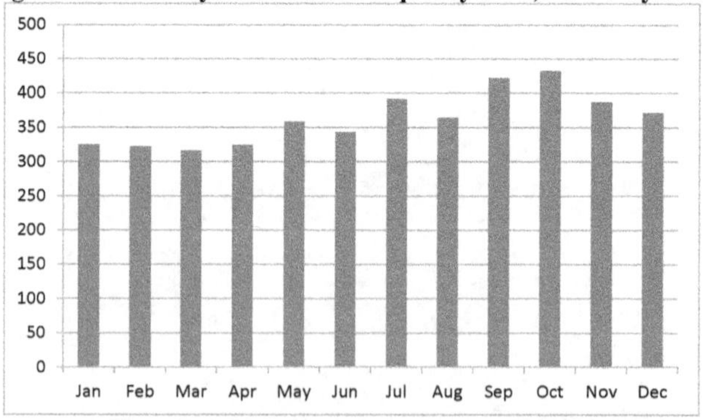

The average size of the 4,355 systems included in our analysis is 4.55 kilowatts; the median is 4.02 kW. The size distribution is shown in Figure 3.7; as might be expected, it is asymmetrical with a tail towards larger system sizes. The predominant number of systems is between 2 and 6 kW, with the largest number between 3 and 4 kW. Anecdotal understanding of the marketplace indicate that the larger systems, particularly those greater than 10 kW, tend to be relatively complex custom installs with multiple roof pitches and perhaps some ground-mounted array; however, the cost per watt, equipment used and energy production for these system are in line with overall trends.

**Figure 3.7. System Size Distribution**

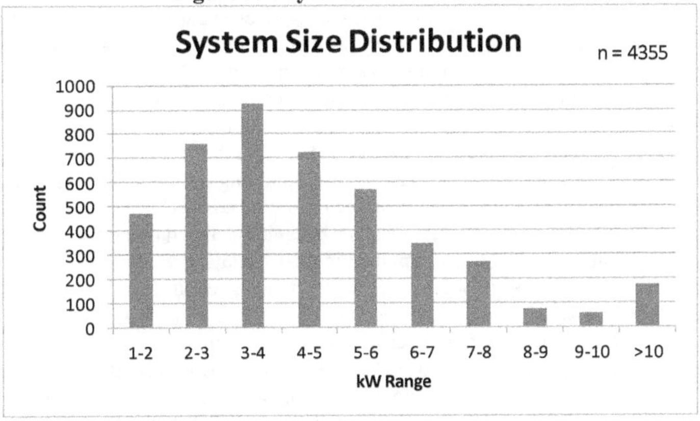


**Figure 3.8. Total and Net Cost per Installed Watt**

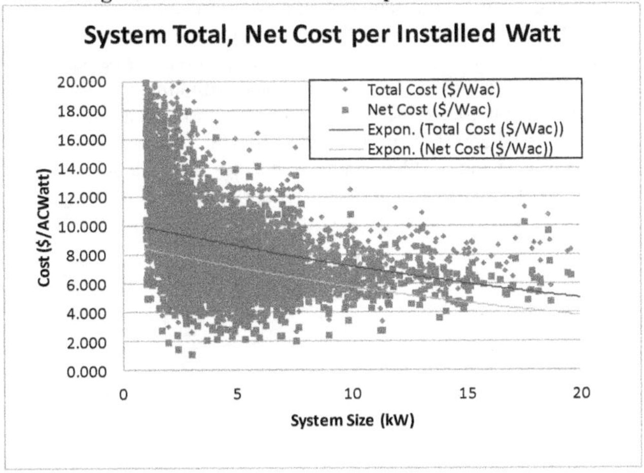

Larger systems tend to cost less per unit of PV capacity; there are some economies of scale in that the sales, admin and labor costs, along with some equipment costs (e.g. inverters) do not rise proportionally with system size. Figure 3.8 shows a scatterplot of system total and net cost in dollars per watt, by system size. We can see wide variation in pricing for smaller systems, and much less for larger systems. The difference between total and net cost is the CSI incentive, which on average brings the cost down by around $2/W.

The evolution of installed solar cost over time is downward. Figure 3.9 shows a 100-system moving average of total and net-after-incentive cost per watt of capacity. Short-term pricing variation is clear with the seemingly erratic movement, which are primarily due to flurries of application from certain contractors. In the early days of the program in fact, total cost per watt stayed relatively flat, while net cost to the customer actually rose as the CSI incentives declined. A brief increase in prices in early 2008 is somewhat difficult to explain, but anecdotal evidence suggests that it is due to inconsistent cost reporting on the part of several installers ramping up new business models aimed at taking advantage of the impending increase in the federal investment tax credit. Specifically, companies developing leasing products—under which the provider rather than the customer owns the system applying for the incentive itself rather than on behalf of the customer—reported as installed costs what were actually total present cost, including discounted future costs (maintenance, service) in addition to the strict year-zero installed cost. This issue of high costs was uncovered by the CSI PAs, and installer behavior changed going forward, but the original period of high reported costs remained in the CSI database. By mid-2008, however, the program was well-established, scale was increasing, contractor difficulty with application and reporting was largely overcome, and PV prices globally had begun to fall.

This downward trend in cost is consistent with a number of studies on experience curves and progress ratios in the U.S. solar market. (Margolis 2002; Nemet 2006; Nemet 2007). PV price reduction is one of the goals of the CSI, and indeed the most recent CSI program evaluation confirm this trend overall (CPUC 2010), though the CSI is certainly not the only driver of price declines in what is a global marketplace. The population of systems considered in this study represents 8% of all the residential systems installed statewide from January 2007 through 2010. Note that the net cost shown here reflects only the CSI rebate; in practice most customers' net cost will be lower, since the bankable value of the solar investment tax credit would also apply for each individual consumer who owns their system: customers with taxable income not subject to the alternative minimum tax (AMT), and who purchased their system, would experience a net cost 30% lower than that shown. Customers with leasing or PPA arrangements may, but will not necessarily, capture such savings: the solar provider has unique pricing flexibility depending on its specific business model.

**Figure 3.9. PV System Cost Evolution by Program Volume, SDG&E Territory**

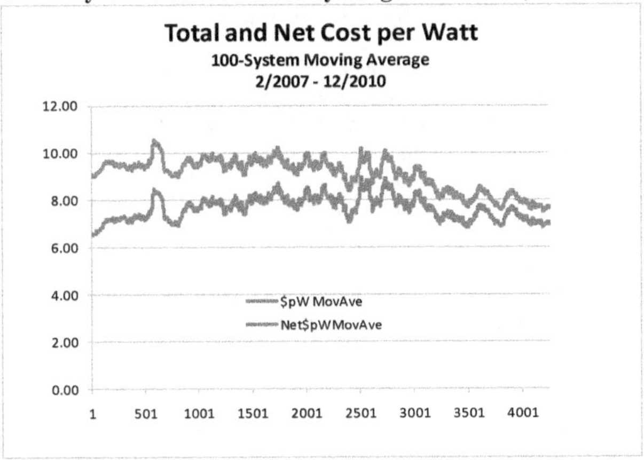


Knowing which customers live in electric-only homes is important for understanding the economic impact of installing solar generation: as explained in the next section, the baseline allocations are larger for these customers. SDG&E serves about three-quarters of its customers with both electricity and natural gas, and the majority of the remaining quarter live in electric-only homes. Customers without utility gas service may utilize propane purchased from an independent distributor, at a cost of 3-4 times that of utility natural gas service (a very small number located in the northern part of SDG&E service territory receive gas service from Southern California Gas Company (SoCalGas)). Figure 3.10 shows the distribution of our CSI participants who are dual-fuel and electric-only SDG&E customers, and essentially reflects the coverage of the SDG&E natural gas distribution networks.

**Figure 3.10. Electric-Only and Dual Fuel Customers**

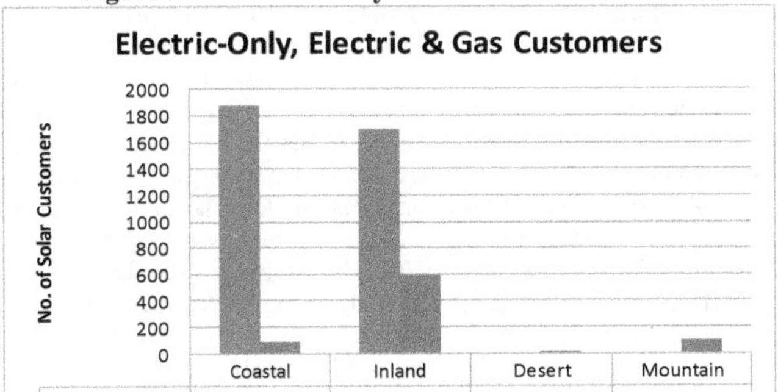


| | Coastal | Inland | Desert | Mountain |
|---|---|---|---|---|
| Electric & Gas | 1878 | 1692 | 0 | 0 |
| Electric-Only | 88 | 592 | 9 | 96 |

### 3.3.2. Consumption levels, System Size and Household Characteristics.

Parcel data from the San Diego County Assessor were provided to the author by the County of San Diego. APN codes were matched for over 90% of the systems in our population. Information was not available for Orange County parcels, which represent 8% of the systems, thus accounting for most of the unmatched systems. Not all fields were available for all parcels, and the data contained evident errors, which were purged. Overall, information for San Diego County parcels enriches the analysis and may contain relevant explanatory power for system sizing trends and behavior responses.

Energy consumption varies with housing characteristics, most basically home size. Figure 3.11 shows the relation between system size and home size: as we might expect, solar system size increases with home area and number of bedrooms. At the same time, there is considerable variation within the population, which gives rise to the opportunity to segment the population to understand the trends.

**Figure 3.11. System Size by Home Area, Number of Bedrooms**

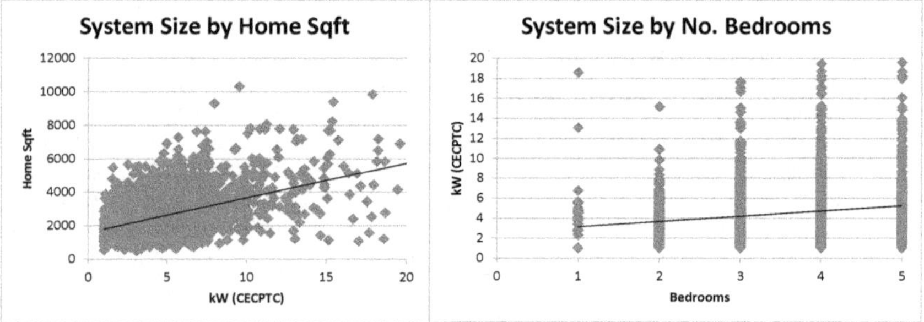


Older homes in the San Diego region tend to be smaller and less efficient, while newer homes, built with newer technologies and subject to building energy codes (California Title 24) for new construction, trend larger but have lower area-normalized electricity consumption. These trends are evident in Figure 3.12, which shows those variables for our study group by build decade. Absolute consumption increases in lockstep with build decade; while area-normalized consumption is progressively lower for homes built in each decade after 1950. Also, the newer the home, the larger the PV system; as we will see in more detail, PV system size correlates strongly with overall consumption.

Lower specific electricity consumption likely has to do both with inherent properties of buildings (less surface area per unit of volume), as well as the onset of building energy efficiency standards in the early 1970s. The upsizing of new homes since 1950 is a well-characterized phenomenon (Calwell 2010; Chong 2010) and is clearly reflected in the solar adopter population. Again, newer homes tend to have somewhat larger solar systems as well, though not fully proportional to their higher absolute electricity consumption.

**Figure 3.12. Electric Consumption by Home Age and Size**

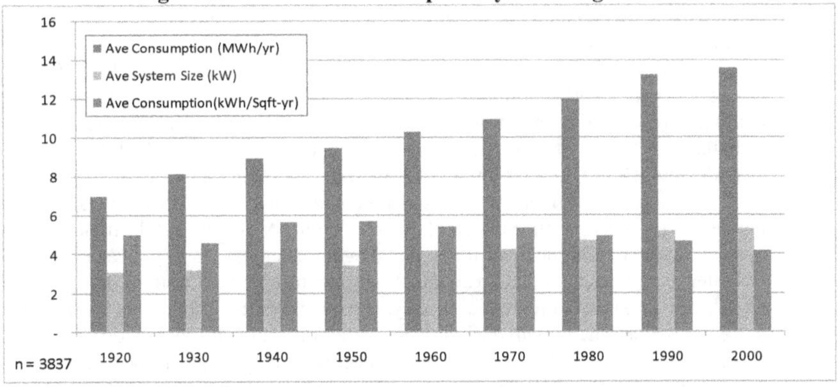


Finally, system size correlates with home value. Figure 3.13 shows that system size increase with assessed property value as shown in the San Diego County Assessor database. To the extent home value also correlates with consumption and affluence generally, this makes intuitive sense. One note of caution, however: in California, assessed property value is not necessarily reflective of actual market value, both since Proposition 13 keeps annual increases in assessed values to a minimum, and given the recent turmoil in housing markets. There are many properties with very low assessed values, certainly many of them much below actual market value, due to long tenure of the current owner. Still, the overall correlation is quite clear.

**Figure 3.13. Assessed Property Value vs. System Size**

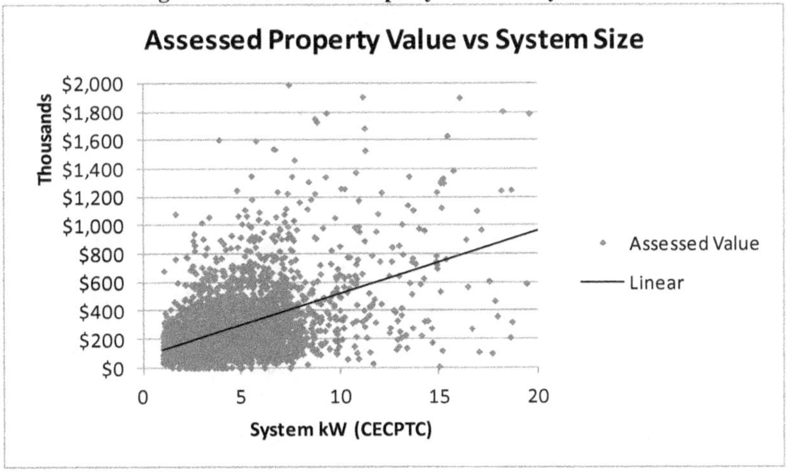

Solar adopters tend to belong to higher socioeconomic strata, though there is some evidence that this is changing. Figure 3.14 shows the percentages of PV adopters in our population in each of the six PRIZM Socio-economic segments supplied by SDG&E with its billing data. We see that the large majority belong to the "Successful" or "Comfortable" categories, with significant numbers of "Professionals" and "Established"—the latter tending to be coastal empty-nesters who own their homes outright. "Young Mobiles" and "Challenged" customers, the two lowest income levels reflected in the PRIZM categories provided by SDG&E, are the smallest adopter groups, at just 1-2% each.

As the most affluent customers with the largest homes, "Successfuls" tend to install the largest PV systems on average—5.3 kW. "Young Mobiles" install small systems on average, with "Established" customers' average system size slightly greater. Interestingly, "Challenged" customers that do adopt PV tend to install larger systems than "Established", likely due to relatively greater occupancy, consumption and utility bills. As solar becomes more accessible, due to both declining costs and innovative business models that include leasing options and PPAs, lower-income homeowners have significantly improved access to solar, since these sellers offer options requiring little or no money down.

**Figure 3.14. Percentage and Size of CSI PV Systems by Socio-Economic Segment**

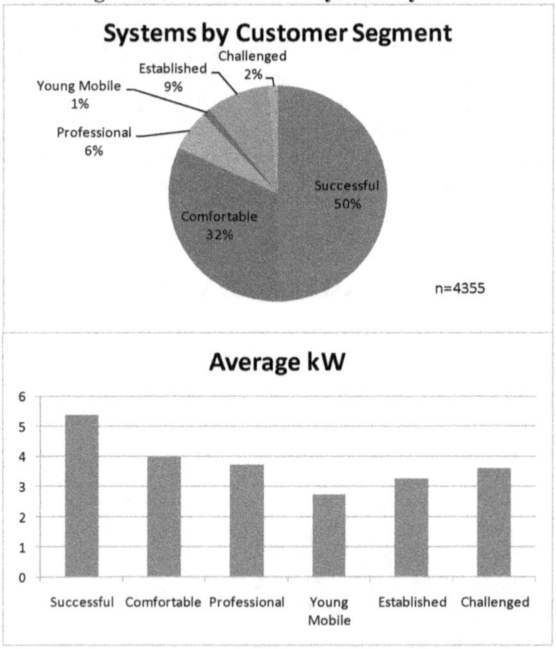


The geographical distribution of solar installs by PRIZM segment is shown in Figure 3.15. Among PV adopters, "Comfortables" and "Successfuls" are rather evenly distributed throughout the region, though "Successful" adopters are less concentrated in the urban center and near-suburbs of the City of San Diego. There, they are somewhat supplanted by "Established" and "Professionals" who, at least among PV adopters, tend to have a more urban orientation. The few "Challenged" adopters tend to be located inland—where home affordability is higher—and where the motivation to reduce energy costs would be strong given high summer air conditioning requirements.

**Figure 3.15. Socio-Economic Groupings of CSI Participants by Zip, SDG&E Territory**

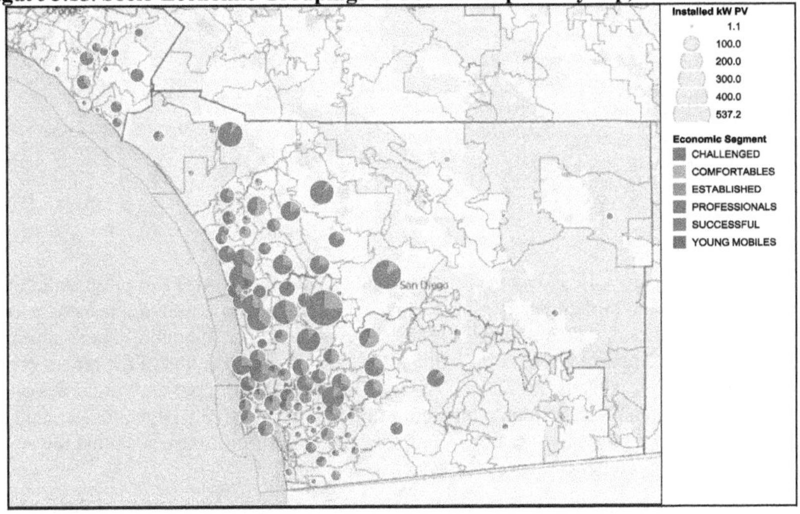


### 3.3.3. Pre-installation electricity consumption of CSI participants

Figure 3.16 shows average daily consumption for our solar adopters during the 12 months prior to PV installation (n varies each month depending on data availability), and that for the average residential customer across SDG&E territory for the same months. The utility-wide averages cover all residential customers, including multifamily apartments and condos which have lower square-footage and generally fewer residents, whereas the CSI population is almost entirely composed of detached single-family homes. Solar adopters indeed on average consume more electricity than the average residential customer. However, the seasonal patterns are clearly evident in both populations: summer consumption is higher than winter, due to space conditioning, pool pumps and other predominantly warm-season loads.

**Figure 3.16. Solar Adopter Average Daily Electricity Consumption**

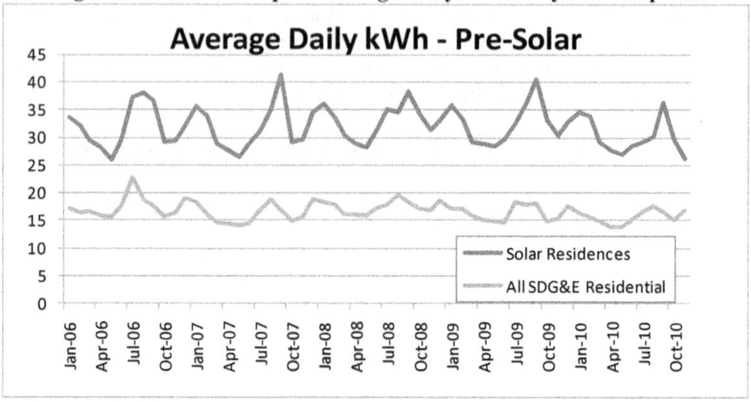


Figure 3.17 shows the relationship between system size and pre-installation consumption, broken out by climate zone. The tendencies are similar across the region and not unexpected, with system size increasing with total consumption. There appears to be a tendency to upsize PV systems in the inland area at the large end of the range, greater than 10 kW. This is likely a reflection of large, relatively new upper-end properties on expansive top-end inland lots, with both high consumption and relatively large areas of land and roof space. Such properties are rarer along the largely built-out coast, such that fewer projects include very large residential PV systems.

**Figure 3.17. System Size vs. Annual Electricity Consumption**

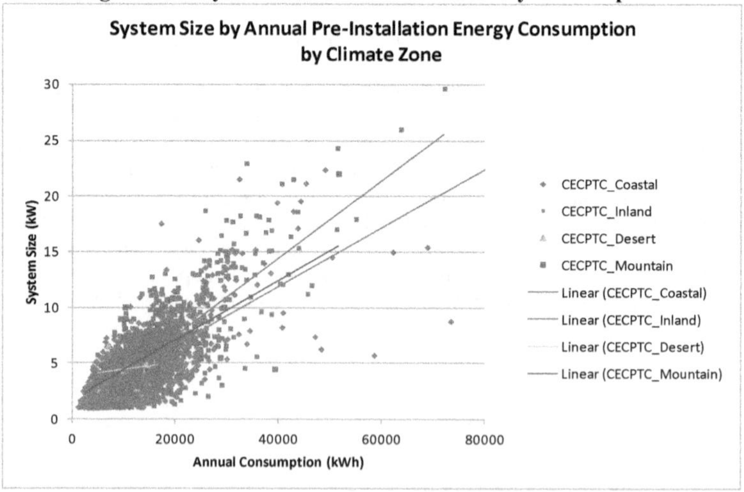

## 3.4. CONCLUSION

This chapter analyzed the solar "value proposition" for adopters in the San Diego region. Solar installations are distributed throughout SDG&E service territory, roughly equally in the Coastal and Inland climate zones. Solar adopters use twice the electricity of the average SDG&E residential customer. PV system capacity correlates generally with electricity consumption level and home size. PV cost per watt of capacity decreases with increased system size, and has been declining generally since mid-2008.

The recent decline in installed cost is a positive indication of the strength and maturation of the solar market. At the same time, risks are present on the horizon in the next few years. Specifically, an accessible net cost to the average customer depends on the policy-driven factors: the federal investment tax credit and net energy metering. As state incentives disappear, these factors play an ever more important role in the viability of solar. First, reduction or repeal of the ITC would increase the customer LCOE by 20-30%. Second, NEM has been a central driver of the small-scale solar market. Rate uncertainty and questions about the future of NEM place into question the sustainability of models that depend upon the gap between retail offset and actual cost of solar generation. The near-term outlook is positive: until residential rates are radically redesigned and/or NEM is modified or repealed, the value of solar for residences utilizing above-average amounts of electricity will remain strong.

# Chapter 4. THE SOLAR SIZING DECISION

## 4.1. INTRODUCTION

This chapter analyzes the predominant practices and trends regarding solar-electric system sizing. The sizing decision is both a first statement about the solar transaction itself, and a key point in an ongoing series of actions by the electric customer, within, perhaps, a sequence of behaviors that will continue after installation of the solar system. Many or most customers may not appreciate the specific details or implications of their solar adoption decision, but understanding these decisions is a critical first step in dissecting adoption trends and determining solar's role in consumption patterns. We are concerned here with the practical decisions being made within the marketplace, whether or not the purchaser him/herself is initially aware of the full array of impacts on overall energy consumption. With this basis of understanding, we can then look at trends in clean energy decision making with a more informed eye, towards designing policies and programs to accomplish specific goals, within California and beyond.

A rational technical-economic decision by a residential user would be to choose a system size that maximizes his internal rate of return. In effect, an economically optimized system would be sized to offset the user's high-tier (expensive) energy use. However, there are many reasons why a system may be sized differently either smaller or larger, from the economic optimal thus defined. A homeowner might choose a smaller system due to limitations in capital availability or feasible roof space, or in anticipation of future energy efficiency investments that would reduce overall consumption. On the other hand, some homeowners wish to offset most or all of their electricity consumption, regardless of whether this is economically optimal, due to environmental concerns, beliefs regarding future electricity prices, contemplated purchase of an electric vehicle, a desire for independence from the utility, or other reasons. Anecdotal evidence in the San Diego region, where the military presence is notable, indicates that energy independence is a relatively strong factor in many adopters' calculus. Solar sales and installation services vary tremendously as well; solar contractors may suggest a larger system than is economically optimal, and may or may not assist the customer to understand the possibility that cost-effective energy efficiency improvements could make a smaller, less costly PV system more appropriate.

The chapter is divided into two parts. First, the methods used to analyze the solar sizing decision are discussed. Second, the results of the analysis are presented.

## 4.2. METHODS

The following plan was constructed and followed in conducting the analysis:

- Model expected PV production for the sizing decision, utilizing typical meteorological year (TMY) solar radiation data. The goal here is to estimate generic output data of the sort that would have been available to the installer and customer during the purchase decision. Thus, TMY data are most appropriate here, since they are what the contractor's model would have used.

For this analysis we utilize the National Renewable Energy Lab's (NREL) System Advisor Model (SAM), for PV production analysis. SAM can provide monthly production estimates based on either TMY or actual solar radiation data, and thus serves the needs of both the pre-installation sizing assessment (using TMY data) and the post-installation production modeling (using actual solar radiation data, which in our case was acquired from a third party). SAM also allows batching routines to be set up via its embedded programming language, which standardizes and speeds modeling and was essential for efficient processing of the 5243 systems in our study.

- For each customer, utilizing the climate zone and appropriate baseline allocation and applicable electric rate, calculate monthly costs of energy purchased from the utility: total, average and marginal costs. This was done for all available utility data, pre- and post-installation, at once for the sake of economy of effort. In this chapter we utilize only the pre-installation cost information.

- Characterize the sizing decision for each household with solar, including an analysis of the utility billing impact expected at the moment of installation. Determine *prima facie* which systems in the dataset are sized economically optimally, "oversized" and "undersized." The result is two unique metrics for each system: first, the anticipated percent of pre-installation load to be offset by the PV system; and second, the "sizing index," which expresses the proximity of the anticipated post-installation utility consumption to the customer's respective cost-effectiveness threshold (i.e. 130%-of-baseline).

- Examine patterns for system sizing and cost, based on installer, pre-installation consumption and cost, customer segment, climate zone, home age and size, etc. The goal is to detect patterns and trends in system sizing.

### 4.2.1. Determining Expected PV Generation

SAM/PVWatts was used to model typical-year monthly expected output for each system, based on that system's equipment and calculated DC-AC derate. PVWatts is the basis for the EPBB calculator, and thus is utilized systematically within the CSI, in addition to any number of additional, often proprietary modeling tools that vendors may choose to use as well. As the industry standard utilized to set production expectations for both vendors and customers, PVWatts output is the most appropriate tool to gauge expected system output in the context of the sizing decision.

SAM/PVWatts was used to estimate the anticipated electrical output of each system in the sample. This exercise was not meant to model actual output, but rather to provide a well-founded predicted output for each system using an analysis similar to that which would likely have been performed during the sales process by the sales agent, contractor, or by a well-informed customer him/herself. Thus, while actual equipment and physical installation characteristics were utilized for each system, the weather data utilized were "typical meteorological year" (TMY) data—the best foundation for predicting average future system output. The exercise was accomplished for the entire group of 5,243 systems utilizing SAM/PVWatts.

### 4.2.2. Anticipated Energy to be Offset by On-site Solar: The Sizing Index

The decision of what size PV system to install is central to the adoption process, and reflects both the interests of the customer and the approach of the sales agent. Solar sellers and/or contractors typically size their proposed systems based on the previous 12 months of utility bills; the proposed system will offset all or part of this baseline, according to the customer's general wishes. The "Percent Estimated Offset" is thus a valuable indicator of the sizing approach for each system. We thus calculate for each system its anticipated consumption offset, in percent of 12-month historical consumption, at the moment of solar installation.

As another, complementary way to characterize the sizing choice, the author developed a "Sizing Index" and calculated it for each system. The purpose of this analysis is to gauge how close the target offset is to a clear and understood economic threshold. We thus relate the anticipated post-installation utility-billed energy (that not expected to be offset by the PV system) to the functional baseline threshold, that is, between Tiers 2 and 3 for each respective customer. The "sizing index" is defined as follows:

$$\text{SizingIndex} = \frac{\text{monthly (consumption} - \text{expected PV generation)}}{\text{Tier2-3 Threshold (kWh/month)}}$$

A sizing index of unity indicates that the installed system would be expected to offset, on average, just enough on-site consumption to land the average net consumption at the Tier 2-3 threshold; the energy to be offset by the PV system would be predominantly from Tiers 3, 4 and 5—that is, relatively expensive. The remaining energy billed by the utility would lie in the near-baseline realm, around 12 cents/kWh—less expensive than that produced by the PV system on a LCC basis.

Further, sizing groups are defined as follows:

**NetZero-:** consistently at or below zero net consumption (sizingindex <= 0);
**NetZero+:** just above zero net consumption (0 < sizingindex <= 0.2);
**Aggressive:** anticipated net consumption less than 70% of the Tier 2-3 threshold (0.2 < sizingindex <= 0.7);
**Economic:** between 70% and 130% of the Tier 2-3 threshold (0.7 < sizingindex <= 1.3);
**Headroom:** between 130% and 200% of the Tier 2-3 threshold (1.3 < sizingindex <= 2);
**PV Limited:** over 200% of the Tier 2-3 threshold remains on the bill (sizingindex >=2).

We hypothesize that these groups would show differing trends that assist us in looking for patterns within the program and/or adopter population.

## 4.3. Results

Figure 4.1 shows a histogram of systems by expected percent electricity offset, based on a full year of utility billed energy consumption immediately prior to solar installation. The TMY-modeled output of each system was compared to the respective customer's billed electricity consumption, to see what portion would have been reduced by the V installation. This is typically how contractors approach the PV sizing decision. We see that expected offset for most systems is between 20% and 80% of total consumption, with a distribution that is reasonably symmetrical. A significant number (443 systems, or 10.8%) are sized to offset more than 100% of existing energy consumption, while a smaller number (60, 1.4%) are clearly constrained in some way, sized to offset less than 20% of existing consumption.

**Figure 4.1. Predicted Percentage Consumption Offset**

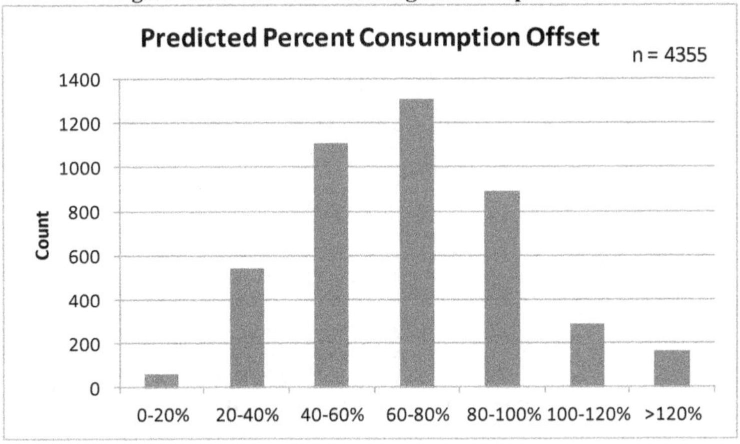


This graph does not tell us, however, about the value of the energy expected to be offset and thus does not reveal detailed strategies in use for the sizing decision; for that we need to look at the applicable electric rate, the baseline allocation on which it is built, and the increasing block (tier) structure that drives the solar value proposition. For simple elucidation of this concept, we utilize the aforementioned Sizing Index.

After subtracting the energy output from the PV system, the remainder would have been left on the utility bill, and billed at the prevailing rate. Indeed, the implicit full-retail value of the energy generated by the PV system, and the residual utility bill that the customer can expect going forward, are among the key pieces of information that a knowledgeable contractor would present to the customer during the sales process. The Sizing Index reveals how close each system is to the critical Tier 2-3 threshold, where the retail offset shows a discontinuity that centrally impacts the economic profile of the system.

Figure 4.2 shows the sizing index (SI) calculated for the 4,355 systems in our study group. A SI of unity indicates that the remaining billable energy from SDG&E, after applying the modeled PV generation, precisely matches 130% of baseline for that customer. We see that a majority of systems are sized to a SI of less than unity, meaning that these systems are sized to displace more than the customer's top-tier energy. About 150 systems have a SI less than zero, which means that at current consumption levels, the system would be producing more energy than the customer actually consumes – triggering a small AB 920 payment from the utility. Overproduction in this way would create a clear incentive to consume more energy, since the marginal cost of doing so would be zero (prior to 2011), or small, on the order of 5 cents per kWh (as of January 2011, when AB 920 went into effect).

Small numbers of systems are sized to leave high-tier energy on the table; this could be due to upcoming efficiency projects, or to customer constraints in budget, roof space, etc.

**Figure 4.2. Histogram of Sizing Index**

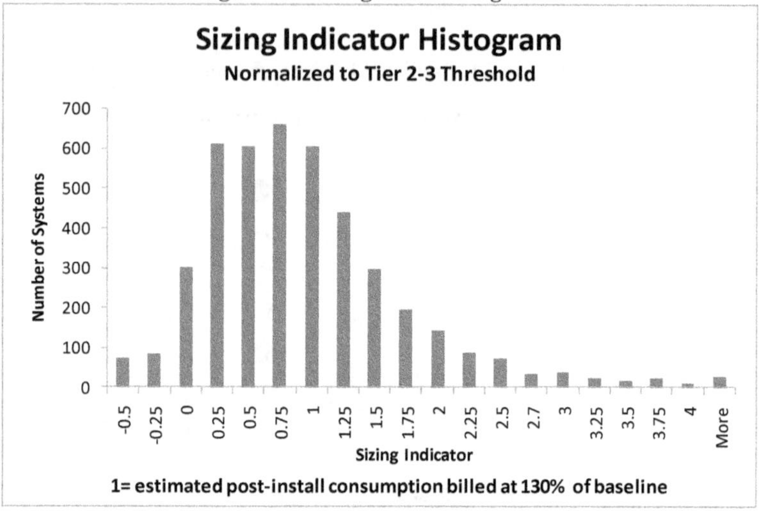


Contractors are very influential in their customers' system sizing decisions. For many solar customers the contractor is the primary source of information and advice during the project life cycle, from sales through implementation. Indeed, the term "contractor" potentially includes several actors along the solar sales and supply chain: the seller, installer or CSI applicant. For our purposes, the Installer and Applicant are the most relevant agents. The Seller makes the main representation to the customer, typically negotiating with the potential customer and closing the deal. The Applicant is the entity making the application to the CSI program for the state PV incentive, usually on behalf of the customer. The Seller and Applicant are usually, though not always, the same entity. Often these are also the same as the Installer, who executes the project. Where this is not the case, the Installer does not control system sizing, acting rather as a representative of the Applicant and/or Seller. We thus focus on the Applicant as the most relevant agent for influencing system sizing. Figure 4.3 expresses total capacity (kW) installed, by CSI Applicant, for the study population of 4,355 systems, sorted by average price per watt. Each column represents the installations of a single Applicant, with the exception of "Self" (all self-installs) and "Small" (all system installed by firms which have done fewer than 5 CSI installs). The wider the column, the greater the total capacity installed by that Applicant. The total capacity represented in the figure is around 20 MW.

Average total cost per watt of capacity varies from \$6 to \$16. There are many reasons for cost differences among contractors, most legitimate such as cost factors related to target market, sales approach, business model and the like. Certainly the high end of the cost range raises flags from a consumer protection perspective: \$14-16/W is a difficult price range to justify even for the smallest (1kW) systems.

There are 14 Applicants with more than 100 installations in our 4,355 systems; these are labeled at the top of the respective column. Including self-installs and small installers brings the total to 16. Average prices for the largest-volume contractors are for the most part in the middle range: \$8-9/watt, with the exception of one large-volume contractor towards the high end. Notably, this company is a pioneer in PV leasing, and likely reports pricing that reflects more than the straight initial installed cost. We will continue to explore the phenomena of residential leasing and PPAs in this chapter and the next.

**Figure 4.3. Average PV Pricing by Contractor**

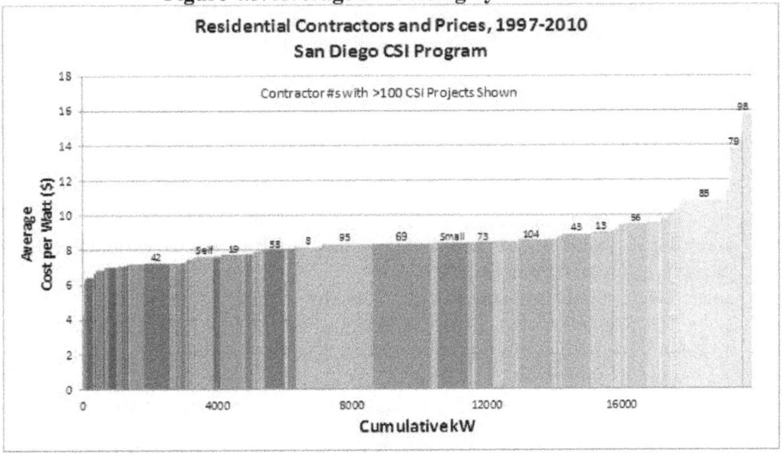


What can we say about incentive levels—do they inspire higher prices and/or larger systems? Figure 3.8 presented the cost evolution, which is generally downward over the life of the CSI and particularly as incentives have declined most quickly. One interpretation is that the incentive encourages or enables higher prices. However, it is difficult to make conclusions about incentives as a driver based on this information; many exogenous factors impact PV pricing, and indeed the global price of PV modules is a central part of declining system prices since mid-2008. An open question, likely answerable only by PV manufacturers, integrator and installers, is how much further can installed costs decline while maintaining the viability of the residential PV supply chain.

Figure 4.4 shows the CSI incentive against system size in kW (left) and against the percent estimated offset (right) for each customer. We see the pattern of clustering at each incentive step in the declining incentive structure of the CSI, with many systems just below each step that for a variety of reasons straddled two or more steps. On the left, we see that system size *per se* does not appear correlated at all with higher incentives: the line is virtually flat. On the right, some effect is visible for small systems, as an influence on the estimated offset. That is, incentive levels appear to have a small influence on sizing for smaller systems, in that adopters may have tended tend to upsize slightly when incentive were high, relative to their existing loads. This makes some intuitive sense: the innovator population – those who stepped forward first, enthusiastically, to install PV – might have been expected to show this tendency. Another way to put this is that as incentive levels have dropped, adopters have opted for slightly smaller systems relative to their existing load, presumably in consultation with their installer.

**Figure 4.4. Impact of Incentives on System Sizing**

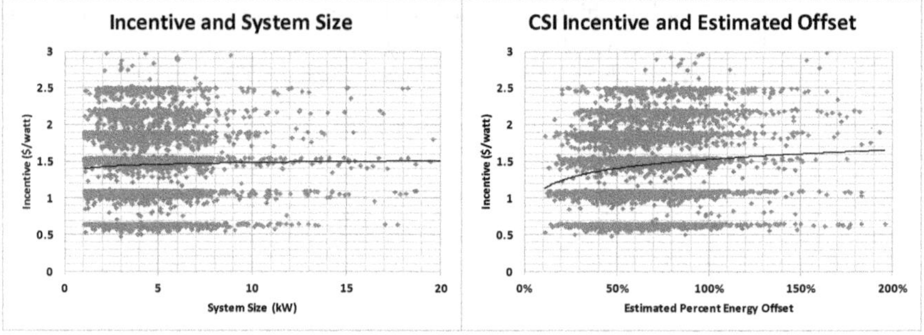


From the customer's perspective, the CSI incentive is just one consideration in adoption. Certainly it enables a lower overall cost, provides a compelling sales message for the contractor, and promotes confidence in the marketplace by signaling state support for solar. The customer's financial decision, however, is based on the overall net cost of the system as s/he understands it. The federal ITC has an important influence on net system cost, particularly after December 31, 2008 when the residential ITC cap was lifted. Figure 4.5 shows net system cost ($ per AC watt) against estimated percent offset for each customer in our study group. Here, clearly there is a correlation between lower cost and higher offset, in the form of a classic demand curve.

A system purchased through a leasing or PPA arrangement presents a different financial decision to the customer than does an outright system purchase. The system is owned by the third-party provider, and the customer pays a monthly charge, based on a leasing payment or on a contractual price for actual energy supplied by the system. The contracts for these 3rd-party-owned installations can be complex, but third-party ownership has been growing tremendously due to the ease of access to these systems: they are often available with no money down and, in most cases, a monthly price that is less than the savings on the utility bill. By the end of 2011, well over 50% of newly-installed PV systems in the CSI were third-party-owned (CPUC 2012), and this percentage has continued to increase since. Compared to ownership, the levelized cost for lease/PPA systems is higher, but adoption via a third-party owner is accessible for a broader swath of the homeowner population.

**Figure 4.5. Net Cost and Estimated Offset**

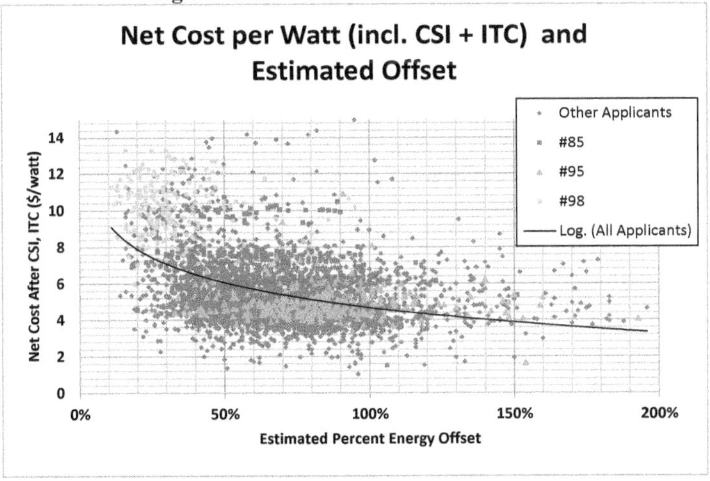


Note also in Figure 4.5 that the systems implemented by three of the largest installers are highlighted. Contractors may have distinct business models, target audiences and sales pathways. CSI Applicant 95 has consistently low costs and a variety of system sizes tending toward larger percentage offsets. At the other end of the spectrum, Applicant 98 installs small, expensive systems. Between these two extremes is Applicant 85. Each of these applicants shows a consistent, intentional approach, and drives the diversity in the growing marketplace for NEM-based solar PV.

An interesting question is: Do 3rd-party-owned systems differ in their sizing from customer-owned systems? This is an important issue as the market expands through innovative business models with vendor-based financing. Costs and sizing may be different for leased versus owned systems. Data for leased systems may not be fully reliable, for at least two reasons. First, the cost data are inconsistent: we have no way to ensure that the correct actual installed cost is reported in the CSI database. Leasing companies tend to utilize sophisticated models since their viability depends on repayment cash flow over the accelerated depreciation period, usually the 5 or 7 years after each installation. Indeed they have tended to be rather aggressive in taking advantage all of the potential tax equity benefits possible. In late 2009, the CSI administrators flagged suspiciously high reported cost data for early PPAs, prompting the PPA providers to change their reporting. Second, whether a system is in fact sold under a leasing arrangement was not directly recorded in the CSI database until 2010, so some leased systems are likely not detected as such in the data.

With these caveats to inform us, Figure 4.6 examines the systems we know to be third-party-owned, alongside the remainder of the study group. The leftmost group is the customer-owned systems; the rightmost group is the third-party-owned systems installed by the largest of the residential PV leasing companies (Applicant #85); and the middle group is third-party-owned systems installed by all other leasing companies. All together the three columns represent our entire study group of 4355 systems. In general, third-party-owned systems are slightly larger, and more than one dollar less expensive per watt, than purchased systems. The third-party-owned systems delivered by Applicant #85, however, show different characteristics: they are slightly smaller and significantly more expensive per watt: $2.40 more than purchased systems, and $3.70 more than the leased systems from other providers.

If we dissect the systems installed by Applicant 85, an interesting story emerges: its non-leased systems (i.e. customer purchased) are reported to have lower prices than leased systems, when the technical characteristics and installation channels of these systems are substantively the same. Figure 4.7 shows this difference in costs clearly; this also explains the multiple clustering of applicant 85's systems in Figure 4.5. The average capacity of the two groups is virtually identical, while the average price differs by $2.85 per watt.

**Figure 4.6. Comparison of PV Sales Models**

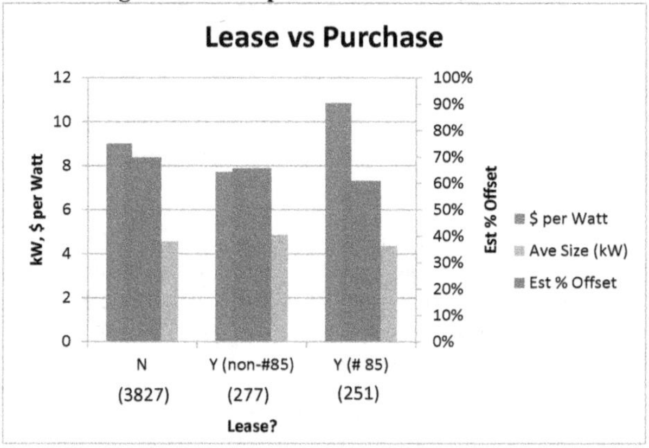


**Figure 4.7. Applicant 85: Leased and Non-leased**

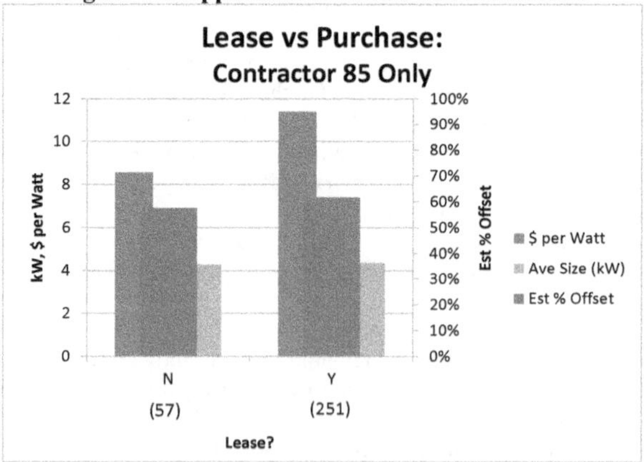

Applicant 85 thus seems to be defining its system leasing business strategy quite precisely: take care to offset only the most expensive energy for the customer, charge accordingly (making sure to charge a rate less than the utility bill saving), and declare retail costs to justify a high federal ITC. A vertically integrated business makes this possible; this company presumably has access to low-cost capital, long-term agreements with various suppliers in order to keep costs down, and controls the supply chain through to its own installer on the ground. Not all leasing companies have this level of vertical integration, and so are comparatively limited in where they allocate costs and profit.

Contractors – those who sell, size and install PV systems—are a key part of the marketplace and fundamentally drive adoption. Their advice directly influences the customer's choice of system, including system sizing. In this section we examine the characteristics of installations done by each CSI Applicant. Over 100 Applicants covered at least five installations under the CSI program in the SDG&E service territory over the study period; another 40 covered less than five each.

Our analysis pays closest attention to the largest solar contractors: those with more than 100 systems in the CSI, in SDG&E territory, for the study period. 14 companies installed at that level of volume; these are labeled by randomly generated ID number in the following figures. We also include self-installs and an aggregated group of the small installers (under 5 CSI installs), for a total of 16 labeled columns. As we will see, there is considerable variation in the cost and sizing trends across the contractor community. We continue to highlight several Applicants for further illustrative discussion: 85, 95 and 98.

Are adopters choosing well-sized systems? Figure 4.8 shows the predicted percentage of energy consumption that would be displaced by PV generation, on average for each installer with 5 or more CSI projects; the top 14 installers are labeled above the respective column, as are Small installers and Self-installs. First, we see that no contractor on average systems to greater than the onsite consumption, which would mean an offset greater than 100% in the figure. Several installers regularly offset greater than 80% of onsite load, while at the other end of the spectrum several tend to install systems covering less than 50% of load.

Sizing strategies vary considerably across the contractor population. As Figure 4.9 shows, the majority of systems has a Sizing Index of between 50% and 100%: that is, thee systems would be expected to displace the customer's utility-based consumption down to between 130% and 65% of baseline. In other words, most systems are sized to offset not only the expensive, top-tier energy, but also some baseline consumption; these systems are less economically cost-effective than the optimally-sized system. For all the metrics we examine—size, offset, and price per watt—Self-installs and Small installers as a group fall in the middle of the range. Self-installs, logically, are somewhat less expensive than average given that labor cost is lower and no markup is included in the reported cost.

If oversizing is occurring, are customers upsizing because solar contractors encourage them to? Most solar contactors are not in business of selling energy efficiency, when in fact a hybrid project with both efficiency and solar may be the optimal solution for some customers—and the one that costs society the least in terms of subsidies and other incentives paid. Our conclusion about sizing of solar systems is important, because understanding consumer motivations can assist to tailor state and federal incentive policies towards the points of maximum leverage.

A priori targeting distinct customer populations; some (98) offer very small systems with a hefty price tag. Others target heavy users for larger systems. Most contractors size systems to overshoot somewhat the top-tier consumption, coming closer to netting out the entire bill. A few contractors seem to be aiming more towards full coverage of the customer's consumption; whether this is self-selection of customers or driven by the contractor is not clear, but the trends do exist.

**Figure 4.8. Predicted Percentage Offset, by Contractor**

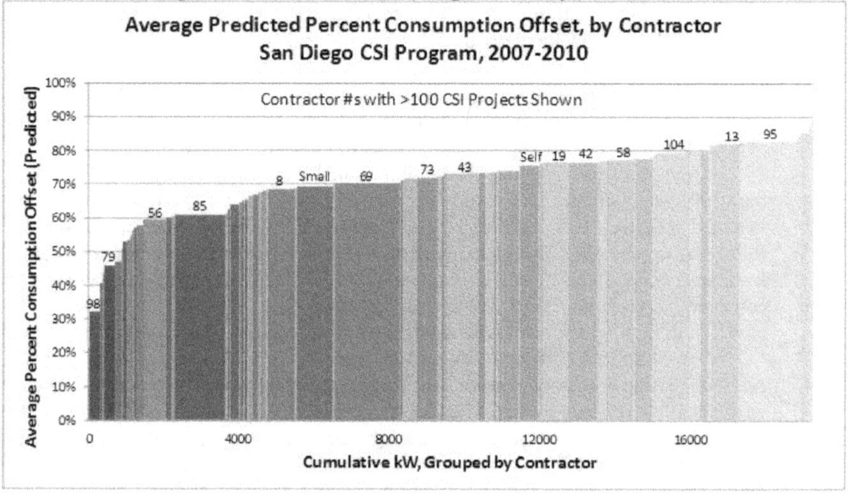


**Figure 4.9. Average Sizing Index by Contractor**

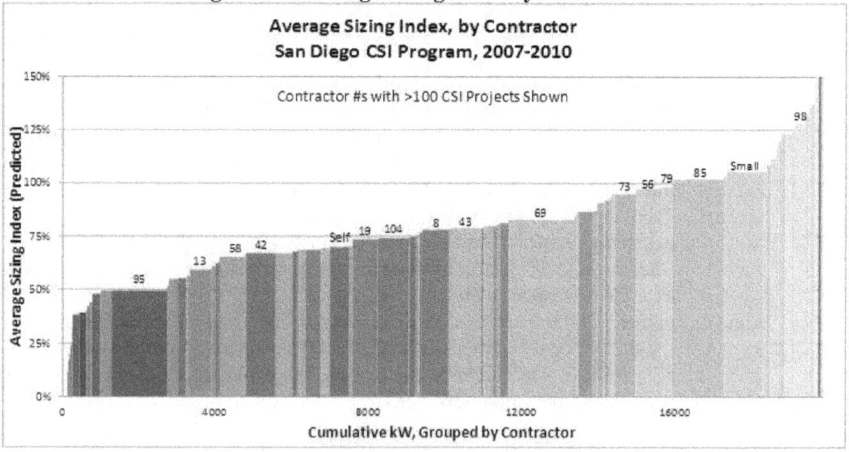

Note that again Contractor 85 is towards one side, in this case precisely at a Sizing Index of 100%, meaning that the displaced energy would have been entirely in Tier 3 and above, while the remaining billable energy from the utility would be entirely in Tier 2 and below. This is unlikely to happen by chance, particularly with a large company installing more than 400 systems in the CSI program. Clearly this installer has made a business decision to optimize the bill reduction for the customer by sizing to eliminate exactly the top-tier energy, and no more. We can see that many contractors habitually size larger than this; certainly there is some pressure to do so based on simple business imperatives—a larger system means more revenue—but , but there may be other factors that explain this skewing of systems larger than the economic optimum, primarily customer preference.

Another question that emerged in our literature review regards the role of utility electric pricing in driving behavior; the behavior of interest in this case is the adoption and sizing decisions. Do high average or total electricity costs directly influence system sizing? Figures 4.10 and 4.11 present, respectively, these costs for the *pre-installation* period, against the estimated % of utility energy expected to be displaced by the system.

Figures 4.10 and 4.11 show the relationship between Average and Total pre-installation electricity costs, respectively, and the proportion of energy to be offset by installations of PV. The results at first seem counterintuitive, in that the less expensive the pre-installation energy, the higher the expected offset. Upon reflection, two things seem probable: first, that the cost of utility energy per se has at most a minimal impact on the sizing decision; and second, that the downward slopes likely simply have to do with norms: smaller consumers (who have lower average and total costs) tend to opt for a "standard" system, which offsets more of their consumption as compared, all else equal, to average or large consumers (who have larger average and total costs). Again, innovators and early adopters might naturally tend toward larger systems in any case.

**Figure 4.10. Average Electricity Cost vs. Estimated Utility Reduction**

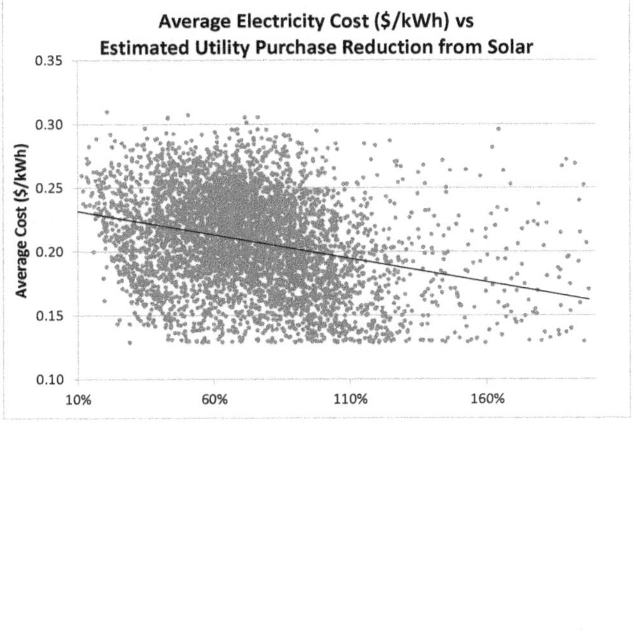

**Figure 4.11. Total Electricity Cost vs. Estimated Utility Reduction**

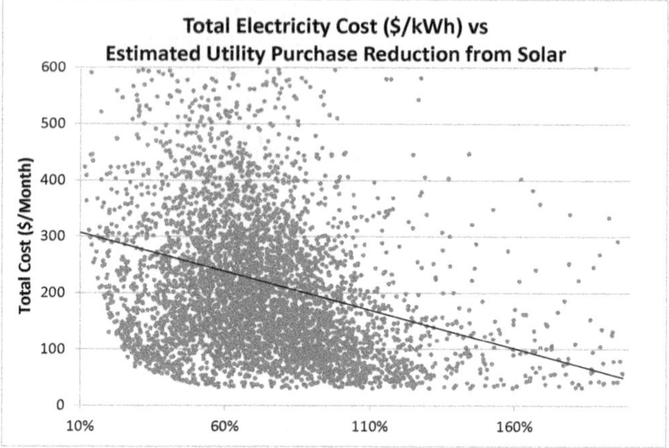


In Chapter 5 we will use the post-installation consumption information to examine the relationship between the pre-post changes utility costs to changes in total electricity consumption. Figure 4.12 summarizes much of what we have learned this in chapter. We can see that average cost is widely variable across contractors, as is customer consumption and contractor sizing strategy. A few contractors present high prices, seemingly undersizing the system and charging the customer a premium. Typically their customer acquisition costs are high, relying at least in part on door-to-door and telephone direct sales. Anecdotal evidence also indicates that these contractors may overpromise, verbally asserting that the system will eliminate the customer's electric bill. At the same time these small systems have a low offset (30% on average), and a sizing index that leaves post-install utility consumption well into Tier 3—sub-optimal system design. Contractor 98 fits this characterization. Indeed, anecdotal evidence indicates that in rare cases contractors may be following an unethical sales strategy: targeting older, less technically-savvy customers with promises of a netted-out electric bill, then installing a small, expensive system that does not meet the promise. In fact, this installer was deemed ineligible for the CSI program, based on evidence of unethical practices.

Another example, at the other end of the spectrum, is Contractor 95, which shows a tendency to oversize systems slightly, though not tremendously more than the average. Costs are on the low end; indeed this contractor seems to be competing on cost to some extent. This company has a good reputation for quality, which has resulted in rapid growth during the course of the CSI.

Finally, the figure confirms Contractor 85's approach to leasing: targeting relatively high energy consumers, installing optimally-sized (smaller than average) systems, and charging higher all-in unit costs through terms of the leasing contract with the customer.

The majority of applicants seem relatively conformist within competitive norms. Self-installs are relatively low-cost systems with medium average size; the larger standard deviation shows higher variation, which makes sense as we might expect this group to reflect heterogeneity. Small installers seem to be working at higher-consuming homes; these projects could be part of remodeling projects, or could be projects done by general contractors for which solar is not a core business. We see high cost variation in that group as well.

**Figure 4.12. Sizing Strategies for Top CSI Installers**

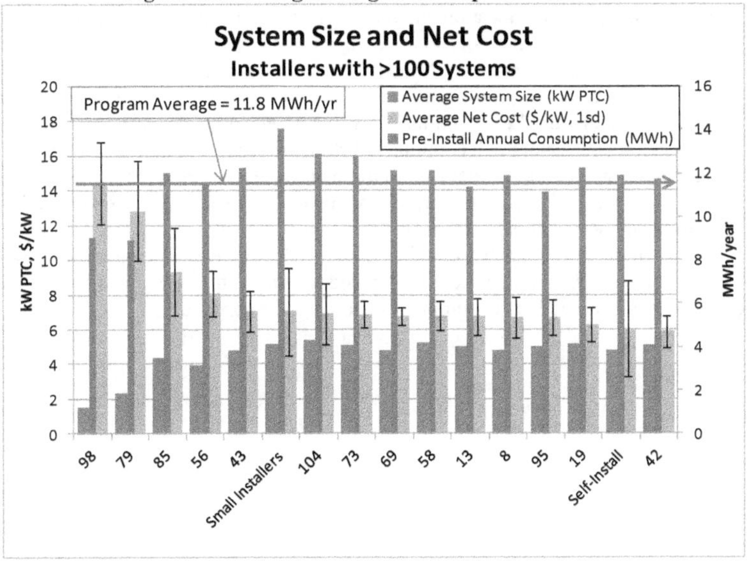


## 4.4. Conclusion

The residential solar adoption decision depends on many factors. Customers bring widely variable interests and knowledge to the solar transaction. Contractors bring varying approaches and business models, which determine the products they offer and what information they present to the customer. Two solar companies seem to focus on the relatively uninformed customer, installing expensive, undersized systems that on average offset just 32% of the customer's utility-purchased energy. Most firms perform well, however, with some distinguishing characteristics within an acceptable range of normal marketplace behavior.

Some installers do tend to install relatively large systems. Some Applicants assert that they assiduously size systems to offset closely to the Tier 2-3 threshold, when in fact the data indicate this is not the case. A majority of companies install system that overshoot the economic optimal. This is likely not an issue of unethical business practices; rather, customers are to some extent comparison shopping and choosing a larger system as the best value.

Clearly both informational and attitudinal factors are at work in the adoption decision. Customers and contractors have varied motivations and influences, with clear responsibility for outcomes on both the interested customer and the sales and installation force. At the same time, it is clear that public policy, in this case in the form of incentives and perhaps other jurisdictional factors (permitting), may impact uptake of new technologies like solar. Finally, we can say that the rational economic actor model is not a well-articulated motivator for solar adoption, but rather it is a general concern mediated by a variety of individual and market-based relationships. Following from this finding, it is very likely that improved education and more available tools and information would improve the quality of solar customer decision making. At the same time, while such transparency would better inform customers about the economic and other impacts of their potential solar choices, as a group they will continue to take this decision within a broader set of views and influences, and will likely continue to exhibit a wide array of sizing and other behaviors. Installation contractors will continue to be the primary informational source for most customers, and should be included in these activities—both in the positive sense of improving their education and professionalism, and through enforcement activities such as post-installation quality assessment.

In the next chapter we look at actual consumption in the post-installation period for these customers, to determine whether, and if so how, the sizing decision might reflect or otherwise be related to consumption patterns going forward.

# Chapter 5. The Effect of Solar Installation on Electricity Consumption

## 5.1. Introduction

In previous chapters we have assembled a significant amount of information about our solar adopter population, looked at the characteristics of the installed systems, the residences where they are located, the contractors who installed them, and the customers' pre-installation consumption levels. This has given us some understanding of sizing decision trends and the potential variables that we might wish to consider going forward. In this chapter we consider how total electricity consumption changes after installation of a PV system, and how the characteristics of the adopter and contractor might influence that change.

Solar adopters with large systems relative to their existing consumption would seem likely candidates to increase their consumption—either as part of a home expansion plan or simply because they are now producing "free" energy and feel decreased urgency to conserve it. Based on our Chapter 4 analysis, we now know which systems are nominally oversized, and can examine actual post-installation consumption to determine trends. While at the customer level such economic "oversizing" may be perfectly acceptable and intentional, incentivizing it via state or federal programs may be seen an inefficient use of ratepayer or public funds. Most simply these incentives are greater for larger systems; further oversizing reduces the customer incentive for subsequent, likely cheaper, energy efficiency and conservation.

Those with small or optimally-sized systems, conversely, would seem most likely to reduce consumption going forward—again, either in a planned fashion or not. The point of understanding the sizing dynamic was to know which households have optimal size: those that do have optimal size preserve incentives to conserve energy. They may adopt technologies or behaviors to further reduce consumption so that their new solar system does cover all their needs. Following diffusion theory, properly-sized solar may be a catalyst for future action. The extended literature provides several possible explanations beyond the rational actor model (or PTEM), acknowledging that behavior emerges from complex socio-cultural contexts. Some people will conserve or adopt efficient technologies for a variety of reasons, which are value-laden and the dissection of which is beyond the scope of this dissertation.

In any given home, mechanistically there may be one of two general dynamics at work. First, the solar system is a discrete choice for the customer, with no other construction project happening at the home. Any increase or reduction in electricity consumption is likely due to weather or behavior change. Alternatively, the solar system is part of a larger project, or series of projects, at the home. In this case, given extensive changes to the home itself, we might expect larger swings in consumption—up or down—around the adoption decision.

What is the impact of installing a solar system on electricity consumption? Does solar installation lead to more or less energy consumptive behavior? In sum: is there a solar take-back effect? This chapter will compare pre-installation and post-installation energy consumption. Further, it will test whether the sizing of the system and certain other variables correlate with or otherwise help to explain the determined changes in energy consumption.

## 5.2. Methods

### 5.2.1. Step 1: Calculating Post-Installation Utility Costs

The average and marginal monthly costs of utility electricity were calculated for every solar customer in the sample, utilizing the actual electric rate schedules in effect for SDG&E service territory each month. These monthly marginal and average costs were grouped for the pre-and post-installation periods for each customer based on the actual billed consumption from the utility. We are interested in the change (overwhelmingly a decrease) in each of these costs from the pre- to post-install periods. 99% of PV customers experienced a lower average cost of energy from the utility after installation. Fully 93% of PV adopters avoided enough energy to move to a lower tier for at least part of the year, resulting in a lower marginal cost as well. Table 5.1 shows these numbers, with the average cost declines, per kWh for average and marginal costs, and total for the utility bills overall. This indicates that after PV is installed, more (often all, as indicated by lower marginal cost) of the customer's remaining utility consumption falls in the lower tiers.

**Table 5.1: Utility Billing Cost Impacts of Solar**

| | Number | Percent of Total | Ave Reduction |
|---|---|---|---|
| **Lower Average Cost** | 2,388 | 99% | $.06/kWh |
| **Lower Marginal Cost** | 2,235 | 93% | $.10/kWh |
| **Total Bill Reductions** | 2,384 | 99% | $153.13 per month<br>73% average savings |

### 5.2.2. Step 2: Production modeling

For each household, the electricity produced by its installed solar system was modeled. Modeling was done using the system's known attributes, including: DC system size; system componentry and the resulting calculated derate factor; tilt, azimuth and mounting type; location (longitude and latitude); and actual weather data from the 10km-by-10km tile in which the respective system was located (Perez/SolarAnywhere). NREL's System Advisor Model (SAM) v.2010.11.9 was the tool of choice for this analysis. Monthly SAM output was adjusted using a factor derived by comparing it to actual production interval data available for the 70 residential solar systems that are part of the performance-based incentive program. This adjusted monthly output was then further modified using the two degradation factors explained above: module "burn-in" and long-term degradation. Modeled PV production was then combined with the monthly post-installation net consumption data from the utility, to produce each household's modeled-total electricity consumption in the post-installation period.

Given that the period between interconnection approval by the utility and the actual interconnection moment varies significantly. SDG&E's interconnection department is fortunately among the most efficient in the state: the interconnection delay is usually less than one week and virtually always less than one month. For our analysis, the month of and the month after (i.e. two months total) interconnection approval are ignored, in order to ensure that the beginning of the post-installation period corresponds to a truly interconnected and operational system for all installations.

The most comprehensive irradiation data available are from the SolarAnywhere database. The data are derived from satellite imagery and available hourly for 10km-by-10km areas throughout the U.S. The author procured this data for the 2006-2010 period for the 78 10km-by-10km "tiles" in which the 4,355 sample systems reside. SAM was then used to model every system during its pre- and post-installation periods, through December 2010. The centerpoints of the 78 weather data tiles are shown in Table 5.2. A geographic representation of these tiles is shown in Figure 5.1.

**Table 5.2. 10x10km Weather Data Tile Centerpoints for PV Production Modeling**

| | Long | | | | | | | | | | | | | | | |
|---|---|---|---|---|---|---|---|---|---|---|---|---|---|---|---|---|
| Lat | -117.75 | -117.65 | -117.55 | -117.45 | -117.35 | -117.25 | -117.15 | -117.05 | -116.95 | -116.85 | -116.75 | -116.65 | -116.55 | -116.45 | -116.35 | -116.25 |
| 33.55 | X | X | X | | | | | | | | | | | | | |
| 33.45 | X | X | X | | X | X | X | X | | | | | | | | |
| 33.35 | | | X | | | X | X | X | X | | X | X | | | X | |
| 33.25 | | | | | X | X | X | X | X | | X | | X | | X | |
| 33.15 | | | | | X | X | X | X | X | | | X | | | X | |
| 33.05 | | | | | X | X | X | X | X | X | X | X | X | X | | |
| 32.95 | | | | | | X | X | X | X | X | X | X | | | | X |
| 32.85 | | | | | | X | X | X | X | X | X | X | X | X | | |
| 32.75 | | | | | | X | X | X | X | X | X | X | | | | |
| 32.65 | | | | | | | X | X | X | X | X | X | | X | X | |
| 32.55 | | | | | | | X | X | | | X | | | | | |

**Figure 5.1. Solar Resource Data Tiles for PV Production Modeling**

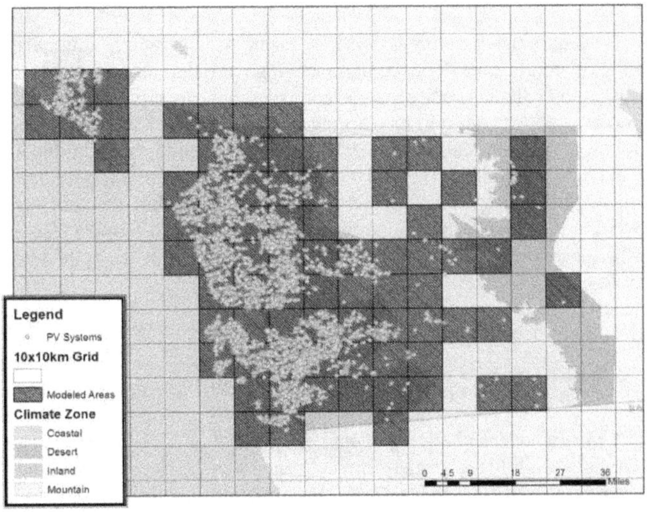


SAM/PVWatts inputs include a DC-to-AC derate factor, for which the CSI DC-AC derate was the starting point. The DC-AC derate is a function of the specific equipment installed in each system, and quantifies the losses incurred during the transformation of the electricity generated by the PV modules to AC electricity adequately conditioned to be injected into the grid. For the CSI group as a whole, the derate factors as listed in the CSI database average 83.1%.

In order to gauge and improve accuracy, PVWatts modeled output was compared to actual production for 59 residential PBI systems for which generation monitoring data were available to the author. The 59 systems showed 4.1% lower production than predicted using the CSI derate, on average. That is, actual production reflected an average AC-DC derate of 0.797 as compared to the CSI-predicted average derate of 0.831. We therefore used an average derate of .797 going forward with the production analysis; i.e. we adjusted the derate factor for each system downward proportionally (i.e. by 797/831). We then reran SAM for all systems, utilizing our adjusted DC-AC derates.

Note that a DC-AC derate of 79.7% is between the CSI-calculated derate and that recommended by NREL, 77%, which is based on long-term study of thousands of systems across the country. The CSI model, while based on PVWatts, the same engine that powers SAM, the CSI model has not, to the author's knowledge, been calibrated to actual output from CSI installations. Our comparison of actual to predicted system output suggests that the CSI method for predicting system output may slightly overestimate production for smaller residential systems, at least in the southernmost part of the state.

Modules degrade over time, in two ways. First, long-term degradation is typically between 0.7% and 1% per year through the module useful life. To adjust for this degradation, three adjustments first, a 0.7% annual derate (equivalent to 0.06% per month after installation) was included in the PV output model, expressed as follows:

$$\text{(Monthly modeled production)}^* \ (1.0006)^{\wedge\text{-(months post-installation)}}$$

Second, the literature shows that during the 6-8 months immediately following installation, modules experience light-soaking degradation, or "burn-in," during which a module starts with a capacity that exceeds nominal capacity, and gradually degrades to approach a capacity close to its nominal by the end of a characteristic decay time after deployment. This effect is particularly pronounced for amorphous silicon modules, which may begin their installed life with a capacity of 10% or more above their nominal (Ruther, Tamizh-Mani et al. ; Weiss, Kratochwill et al.), while mono- and poly-crystalline modules show 1.7% burn-in over a similar period (Ruther, Tamizh-Mani et al. ; Gostein and Dunn). This factor is captured by an additional capacity term with an exponential decay function as follows:

$$\text{Burn-in as percentage of nominal capacity}^* e^{\wedge\text{-(months post-installation/burn-in period in months)}}$$

This term decays to 0 (i.e. no additional burn-in) after the decay period.

Quality of installation matters. We see from the PBI data that systems installed later tend to have slightly higher performance, equivalent to 2% greater initial output for each year subsequent to 2007 that a given system was installed. This finding is consistent with other examinations of the CSI installed base and is uniform across the state (Itron 2010). Reasons for this could be higher-quality installations as the market scales up and is professionalized, and improved equipment specifications. We have captured this trend by adding a 2% annual improvement (0.167% per month) in system output for systems installed after January 2008, which encompasses 90% of all system in our study group. In this way a system installed in January 2010 would have 4% higher production than one installed in December 2007, all else equal.

These three factors were used to correct the SAM output to better reflect the actual equipment and installation conditions in our population. Measured production and modeled production are shown in Figure 5.2 for the 59 systems utilized for this calibration exercise. Also shown in the figure is the monthly difference between modeled and measured output. Overall, modeled production is within 0.02% of measured output for these systems for the months included, which included at least one year pre and post for all 59 systems.

**Figure 5.2. Measured and Modeled Production for 59 PV Systems**

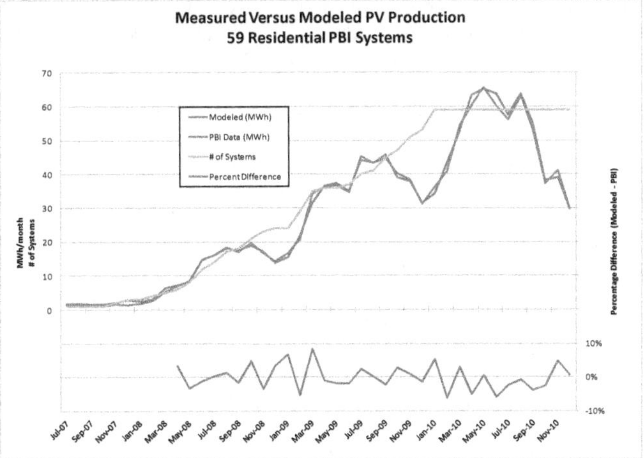


Note that the model shows comparatively smaller differences in summer, where a majority of solar energy is actually generated; this makes intuitive sense as edge effects such as shading and weather will have lower impacts in summer when the sun is higher in the sky and weather is more consistent. As we might expect, the differences narrow somewhat as more systems come into the analysis.

### 5.2.3. Step 3: Weather Impact on Consumption

To capture the impact of variable weather, particularly the effects of cooling loads, on consumption, monthly cooling degree-days (CDD) for each system were incorporated into the data set. Specifically, monthly average temperature data from the National Oceanographic and Atmospheric Administration (NOAA) were used to generate monthly CDD for each system location.[25] Specifically, monthly CDD numbers were calculated for each system using distance-based weightings, through a process called

---

[25] NOAA National Climatic Data Center, Online Climate Data Directory, http://www.ncdc.noaa.gov/oa/climate/climatedata.html

"kirging": the three closest NOAA sites to each PV installation were determined utilizing spatial analysis tools by overlaying the NOAA stations onto a map of the study group installations. The site-specific monthly CDD figures were incorporated as fields in the respective monthly records for each system over the entire 2006-2010 study period. The monthly figures were rolled into annual figures for the purposes of our analysis.

### 5.2.4. Step 4: Pre-Post Comparisons

With the data generation and assembly done, we step next to the pre-post comparisons that will help answer the question: is there a take-back effect around residential PV adoption, and if so what are its characteristics? We first look at consumption at inland and coastal adopters over one, two and three years after PV installation, understanding general trends. We then break down the data to examine other variables such as sizing behaviors; pre-installation energy use, installation contractor, etc.

## 5.3. Data Description for the 5-Year Study Period

As we saw in Chapter 3, 5,243 residential NEM systems were matched to CSI participant data, with various subsets of the total then matched to other datasets such as monthly utility-based electricity consumption, assessor data and the like. When excluding new construction, errant non-residential, and other customers with net negative monthly consumption prior to PV installation or very low consumption, the sample was reduced to 4,445 systems. Twelve (12) full months of pre-installation utility consumption data were available for a final sample of 4,355 systems.

For this chapter's analysis, we focus on the systems for which at least 12 months of pre-installation and at least 12 months of post-installation consumption data were available. Longer-term trends may be visible in the smaller groups of installations with multiple years of post-installation utility consumption data. Numbers of systems with the applicable periods of post-installation data are shown in Table 5.3.

**Table 5.3. Sample Sizes for Post-Installation Consumption Analysis**

| Months Post-Install Energy Usage Data | Number of Systems |
|---|---|
| 12 | 2,410 |
| 24 | 716 |
| 36 | 224 |

## 5.4. Results: Consumption Trends for Solar Adopters

The three graphs in Figure 5.3 show pre- and post-installation aggregate consumption and PV generation for the adopter groups for which one, two and three years, respectively, of post-installation utility consumption information was available.

**Figure 5.3. Aggregate Consumption, Pre- and Post-installation**

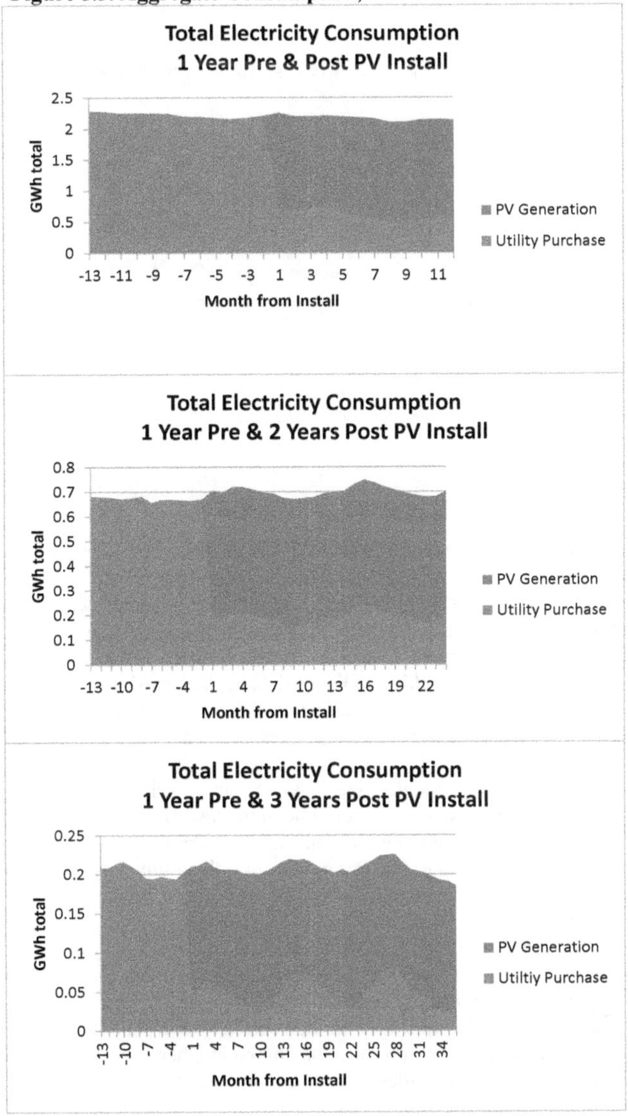


The reason for the seasonal undulation likely has at least partly to do with the seasonality of installation, as we saw in Chapter 3. The group of 2,410 systems in our reduced group exhibits the trend of fall installations even more clearly than the full 4,355-system study group, as shown in Figure 5.4. This pattern carries forward for each system and for the group as a whole.

**Figure 5.4: Monthly Installations for 2,410 PV Systems**

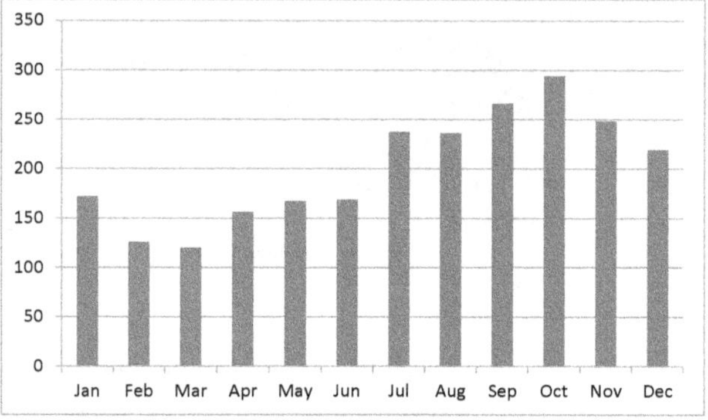


### 5.4.1. Example Homes

An illustrative example will help understand the basic variations we see in consumption changes after PV adoption. Figure 5.5 shows monthly energy supplied by the utility and generated by rooftop PV system for two homes located in San Diego County on which PV was installed in fall 2008. The pre-installation consumption is known, and the post-installation consumption was modeled using SAM, with actual system characteristics and location-specific monthly irradiance data for the post-installation period.

The homes have similar pre-installation consumption, around 600-800 kWh per month on average for the previous year, with peaks around what appear to be the holiday months. One happens to be in the coastal zone, the other inland. The first customer, on the left, installed an "economically-sized" system: one sized to offset existing consumption such that the remaining consumption would lie in the lowest two tiers in the applicable DR SDG&E rate. After installation, this customer's overall electricity consumption declined by around 20%, resulting in low consumption from the utility, largely in winter when PV production is lowest. Just one month in the two years after installation—in the second year—saw net excess PV production.

The other customer, in contrast, installed a larger PV system, sized to offset most of the home's consumption. Rather than decreasing consumption after the PV installation, this customer increased consumption by around 35% over the next two years. Several months of net excess consumption appear in the first spring after installation; the second year sees no such excess production, as consumption climbed higher. Given that this is a coastal customer with generally modest air conditioning needs relative to inland customers, we might anticipate that the increase has a more broadly behavioral origin. We do not, unfortunately, have data to establish causality here; we will examine overall patterns and try to make general conclusions.

**Figure 5.5: Example Homes with Distinct Post-Installation Behavior**

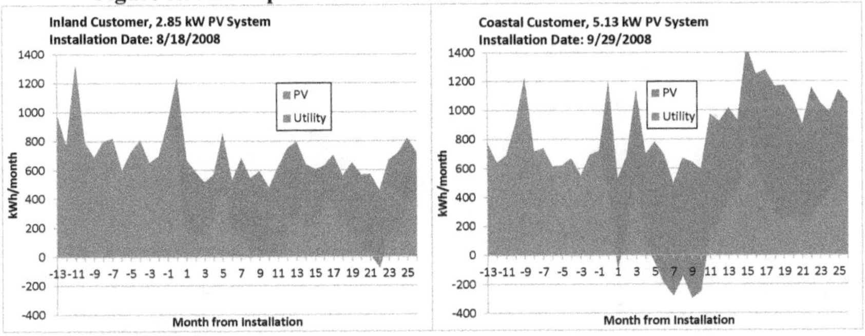


By performing this analysis for the entire sample of 2,410 systems for which at least 12 months of pre- and post-installation utility data are available, we seek to identify patterns and begin to understand overall trends.

### 5.4.2. The Impact of Weather

Residential energy consumption results from a combination of behavior and climate. Weather influences are important and affect consumption directly, even in a mild climate such as coastal San Diego's, but more so inland where cooling is a more important end use. Figure 5.6 shows the monthly area-normalized consumption for coastal and inland solar homes, against CDD for the same groups. The post-installation periods had milder weather which complicates interpretation somewhat. The slight post-installation downward trend seems to hold here as well, though for inland homes the change appears especially small: seemingly, inland PV installations had little effect on consumption since both pre- and post-installation specific consumption fall on a similar trend line. Coastal installations, however, show a somewhat different story: the slope is steeper for the post periods, suggesting a roughly 20% lower baseline consumption after PV installation.

**Figure 5.6. Monthly Average Area-Normalized Consumption vs. CDD**

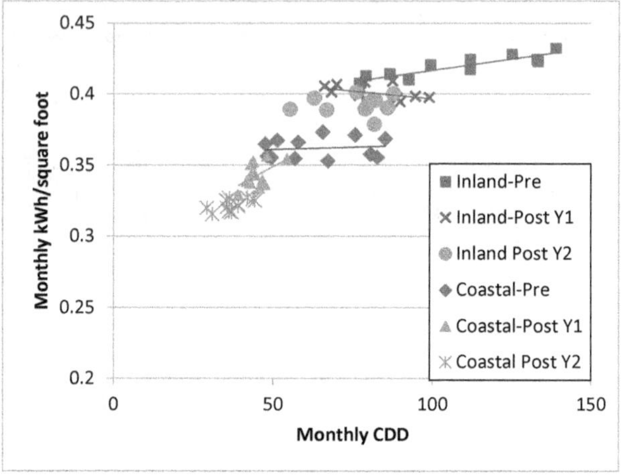


Another potential reason for the lower specific consumption in the post-installation periods emerges when we look at the evolution of the installed population. Figure 5.7 shows a chronological 200-home running average of specific electricity consumption, for the year immediately preceding installation. This metric increases over time by about 10% from early 2007 to the end of 2009. Given that the second and third years of consumption data are only available for homes where PV was installed near the beginning of this period, these latter years will skew low in terms of area-specific consumption.

**Figure 5.7. Pre-PV Consumption, kWh/sqft-month, 200-home running average**

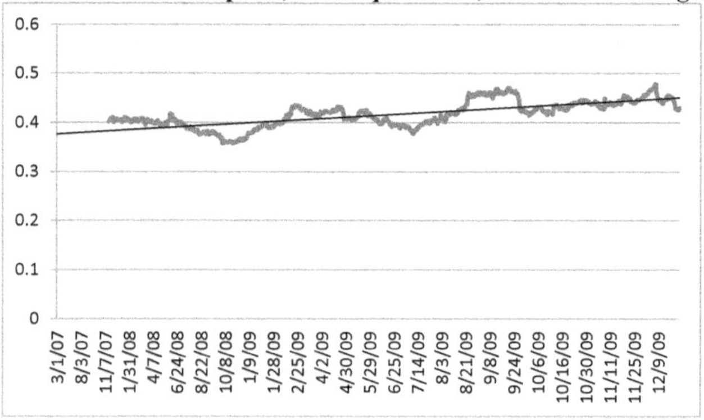

### 5.4.3. Overall Trends

In answering the question of whether a solar takeback effect exists, it is fundamental to look at overall patterns. We added pre- and post-installation utility billed electricity to the modeled PV generation to obtain total consumption for each system. We removed the month on either side of the utility interconnection approval date to avoid noise in the data around the actual installation date. We then added 12 months at a time in the post-installation period, to obtain as many annual totals as possible for each system. Finally, consumption for each year was normalized to the pre-installation year.

Figure 5.8 shows the result: percent consumption by year relative to the pre-installation year, for post-installation years 1, 2, 3 for coastal and inland systems. We focus on system in the Coastal in Inland climate zones; the 2350 systems are the vast majority of the total in our overall study group. The number of systems for which year-2 and year-3 data were available are shown in the data table below the figure.

Several points deserve mention. First, year 1 shows decreased consumption for both inland and coastal, while the second and third years show some bounceback. This decrease could possibly be due to project-related consumption decreases at some of the participating homes, though effort was made to cull such customers from the study group. Second, CDD were highest in the pre-installation year, such that all else equal we would expect to see declining consumption in subsequent years, especially inland where cooling loads are a greater proportion of overall consumption. Indeed this pattern holds for Year 1. Years 2 and 3 show increased consumption, especially inland, while average CDD in those years are fewer than the pre-installation year.

**Figure 5.8. Electricity Consumption Trends for Solar Adopters**

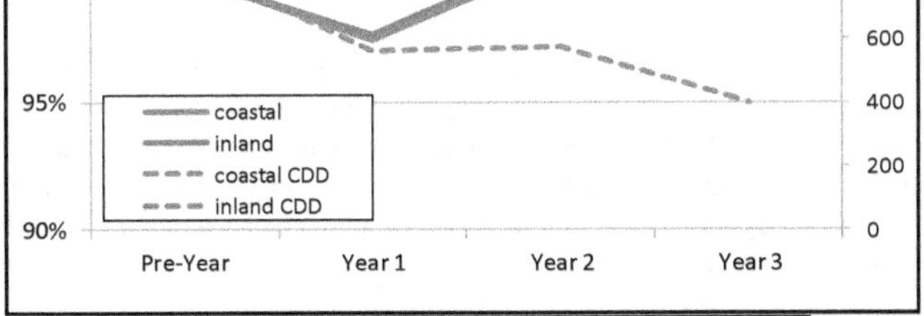


| n | Pre-Year | Year 1 | Year 2 | Year 3 |
|---|---|---|---|---|
| coastal | 1142 | 1142 | 365 | 96 |
| inland | 1208 | 1208 | 332 | 118 |

While our sample sizes for years 2 and 3 are smaller than for year 1, we are left with the suspicion that long-term consumption after PV installation may well be higher than in the pre-installation period. In any case, a clear conclusion is that whether we have a "double dividend" or a takeback effect, the percentage change is small on average, certainly less than 5%.

### 5.4.4. Subpopulation Behaviors

How many reduced energy consumption; how many increased? Based on the available post-install data, of the 2,410 systems in our study group, 1,544 (64%) reduced and 866 (36%) increased overall electricity consumption as compared to the 1-year pre-install period. Those who increased tended to do so by 16-20%, while those who decreased Overall, adopters decreased consumption slightly in the first year after installation, and increased slightly in subsequent years such that, on average, consumption increased by around 2% in the second year after PV was installed. These results are shown in Figure 5.9.

**Figure 5.9. Post-Installation Consumption Changes**

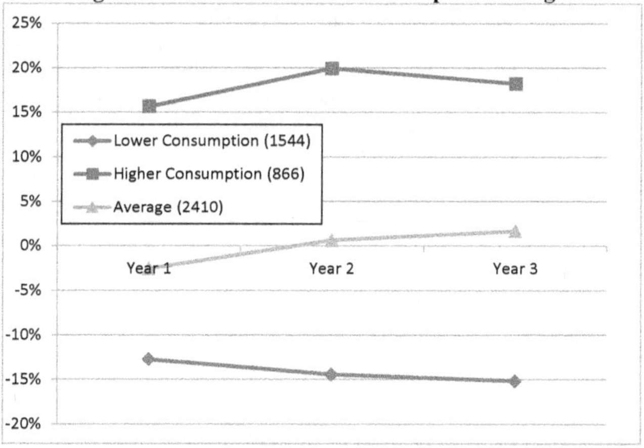


Figure 5.10 presents the ratios of post/pre consumption for all 2,410 systems, sorted from smallest to largest. We see that the majority of adopters' post-installation consumption is within +10% and -15% of pre-installation consumption levels. These changes are within natural year-to-year variation in energy consumption. At either end, however, we see increasing divergence in the post-installation period, and we categorize these adopters as Increasers and Reducers.

**Figure 5.10. Percent Change in Electricity Consumption After PV Installation**

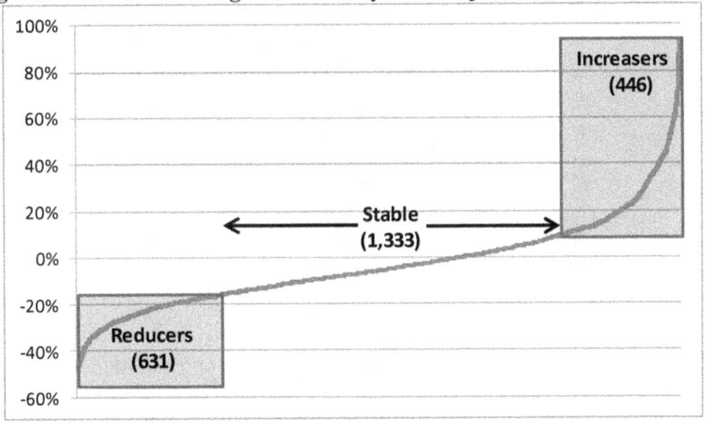


Is there a relationship between system sizing and post-installation consumption? In Figure 5.11 we see that adopters of smaller systems—meaning ones sized to offset less of the customer's utility consumption—have a greater tendency to decrease consumption after installation; the sloped trendlines indicate this. Those installing larger systems tend to increase consumption. We cannot determine causality with the available data. However, this makes some sense from a rational perspective, in that homeowners planning efficiency measures along with their solar installation would likely account for this when purchasing the PV system. Those more interested in covering most or all of their consumption may not be interested in reducing consumption, or may also be involved in home expansion or other energy intensive activities, for which they also may be planning.

Our consumption categories—Reducer, Stable and Increaser—are useful for examining pre-post trends. Figure 5.12 and Table 5.4 show the post-installation percent change in consumption for these three categories, broken out by sizing category. The underlying figures are shown in the table below.

Those with larger systems tended to increase consumption: more than 50% of NetZero- homes are Increasers. Increasers (those whose consumption grew by more than 10% after PV was installed) display behavior that is clear and explainable: with the exception of the smallest ("PVLimited") systems, the larger the system relative to pre-installation load, the more the user increased consumption in the post-installation period. For example, Increaser homes with NetZero- systems—sized to meet more than the user's pre-PV electricity needs—increased consumption by 32% on average, more than those with smaller systems.

At the other end of the sizing spectrum we see similar patterns: Economic, Headroom and PVLimited sizers are much more likely to become Reducers (PV adopters whose energy consumption dropped by at least 15% in the post-install period).

**Figure 5.11. Predicted Offset vs. Actual Post-Install Consumption Change**

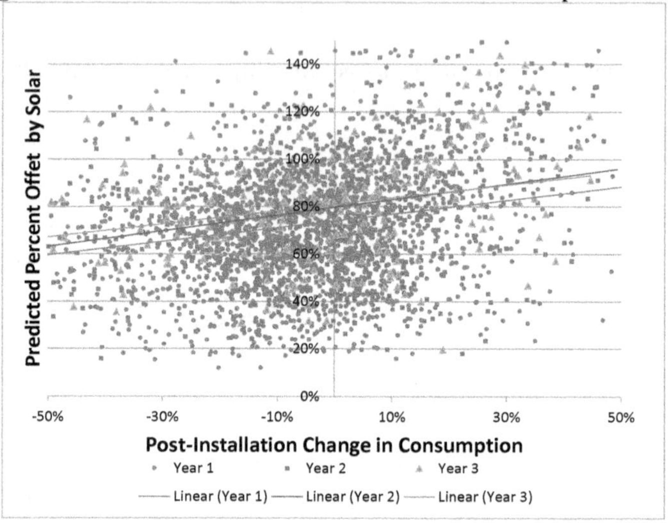


**Figure 5.12. Sizing and Consumption Categories**

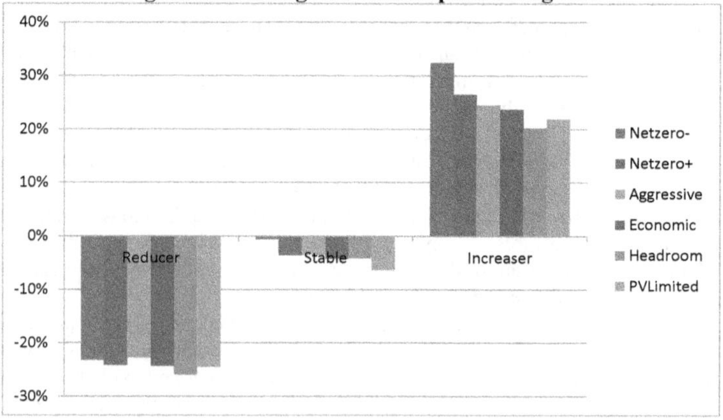

**Table 5.4. Sizing and Consumption Categories**

| *Percent Change* | Reducer | Stable | Increaser | Mean |
|---|---|---|---|---|
| Netzero- | -23.2% | -0.6% | 32.4% | 13.7% |
| Netzero+ | -24.2% | -3.6% | 26.5% | 1.2% |
| Aggressive | -22.8% | -3.5% | 24.5% | -3.8% |
| Economic | -24.3% | -4.2% | 23.7% | -6.7% |
| Headroom | -26.0% | -4.1% | 20.2% | -10.3% |
| PVLimited | -24.5% | -6.3% | 22.0% | -9.5% |
| Mean | -24.1% | -3.8% | 26.4% | -3.5% |
| ***Frequency*** | **Reducer** | **Stable** | **Increaser** | **Total** |
| Netzero- | 25 | 90 | 118 | 233 |
| Netzero+ | 46 | 155 | 76 | 277 |
| Aggressive | 201 | 443 | 130 | 774 |
| Economic | 190 | 407 | 78 | 675 |
| Headroom | 105 | 157 | 22 | 284 |
| PVLimited | 64 | 81 | 22 | 167 |
| Total | 631 | 1333 | 446 | 2410 |

Figure 5.13 presents another way to look at these trends, by comparing the Sizing Category makeup for each of the three consumption groups. Aggressive sizers are well-represented across the consumption groups. Those who increase consumption more than 10% after PV adoption are disproportionally from the NetZero categories; those who reduce by more than 15% are more likely to have made more conservative sizing decisions, as represented by the PVLimited, Headroom and Economic categories.

**Figure 5.13. Post-Install Consumption Bins by Sizing Category**

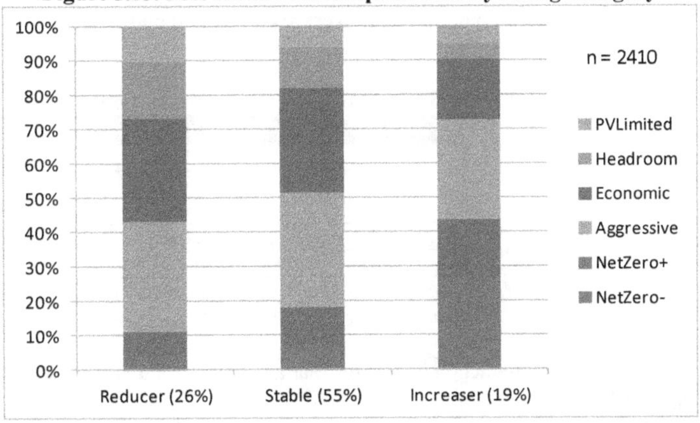


Clearly for each adopter, there are many factors which influence both system sizing and consumption itself, most of which we will not know. At the same time, as we have seen, the contractor has a major influence on the size of the system installed: to the extent the homeowner's choice is not fully informed, s/he may choose a system larger than the optimal. Such "oversized" systems may be an artifact of the solar market's dynamics rather than a well-informed customer decision. Figure 5.14 shows the proportions of our three post-installation consumption categories for each of the top Applicants described in Chapter 4.

**Figure 5.14. Pre-Post Consumption Change by Applicant**

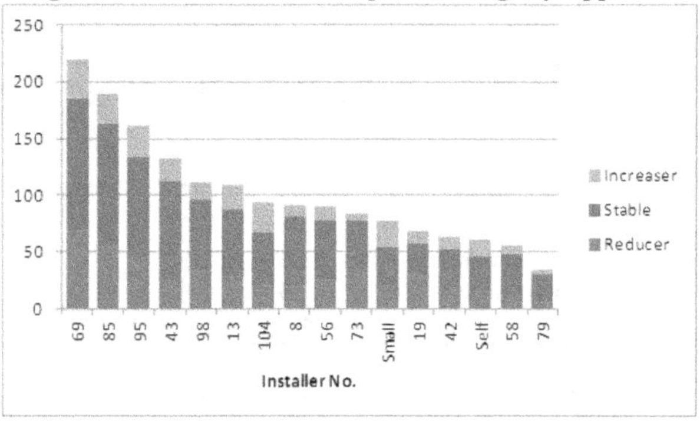


### 5.4.5. Carbon Impacts and REC Production

Finally, it is worthwhile to analyze the carbon reductions associated with PV installations included in this study. Solar produces zero carbon, and offsets electricity that would otherwise be procured by the utility—electricity that has significant carbon content. We utilize SDG&E's reported yearly average electric carbon content for this analysis. Annual $CO_2$ content through 2010 is shown in Table 5.5.

**Table 5.5. Carbon Content of SDG&E Power Mix**

| Year | kg $CO_2$/MWhe |
|---|---|
| **2006** | 354.90 |
| **2007** | 366.49 |
| **2008** | 335.93 |
| **2009** | 327.50 |
| **2010** | 321.17* |

**Not published as of this writing; estimated assuming a linear path to 2013 20% RPS compliance*

The carbon reduction impact of solar adoption for individual users is dramatic. Figure 5.15 shows the monthly average $CO_2$ emissions for the 2,410 homes for which at least one year of pre- and post-installation consumption data were available. The number of systems included for each month is shown for reference; we have 12 months of post-install data for all the system included, but each subsequent month there are fewer systems included in the analysis. The averages do remain relatively stable as the pool of homes decreases. Emissions were reduced by 72%, from over 300 kg $CO_2$ per month per home to under 100.

**Figure 5.15. Electricity-related $CO_2$ Emissions for PV Adopters**

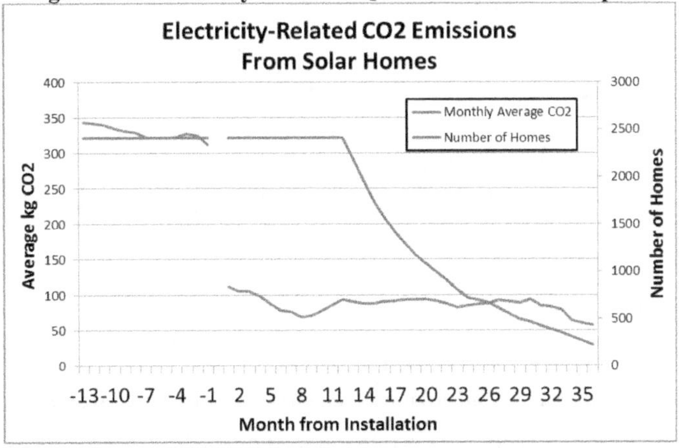


We first model the production of each of the 5,243 PV systems in our study group, by extending the production modeled with SAM through the year 2030, utilizing an annual derate of 0.7%. We then assign a yearly carbon intensity factor to each year's production, discounting to the present as appropriate, as described below.

In order to determine the cost of avoided $CO_2e$ by offsetting electricity otherwise procured by the utility, we must estimate the carbon content of the utility power mix into the future. We assume that SDG&E will meet its RPS obligations, currently to reach 33% by 2020, and that these requirements increase to 40% by 2030, as seems likely. The resulting 2030 carbon content would be approximately 497 kg $CO_2$/MWhe. The modeled numbers were utilized in the carbon costing exercise that follows; the projection is presented in Figure 5.16.

The evolution of the cost of carbon abatement through residential PV installation can be seen in Figure 5.17. Three separate costs are presented: the CSI incentive (blue), the NEM additional cost of procurement (green), and the federal ITC (red). Note that California electric ratepayers cover the costs of both the CSI incentive and the net cost of NEM, while the federal taxpayer covers the cost of the ITC.

**Figure 5.16. Projected $CO_2$ Content of SDG&E Power Mix to 2030**

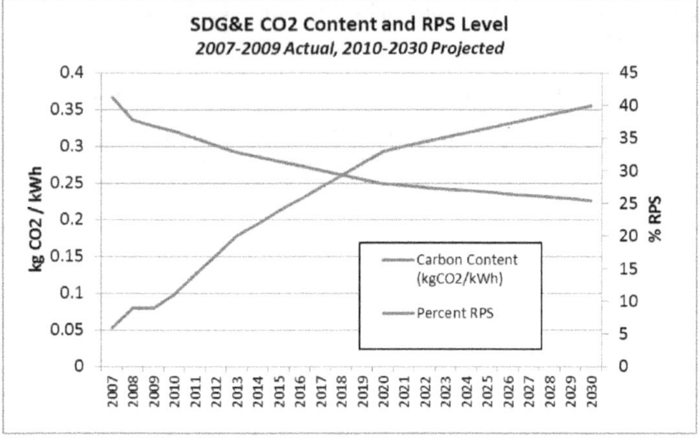


**Figure 5.17. Residential PV Systems Cost of $CO_2$ Reductions Through 2030**

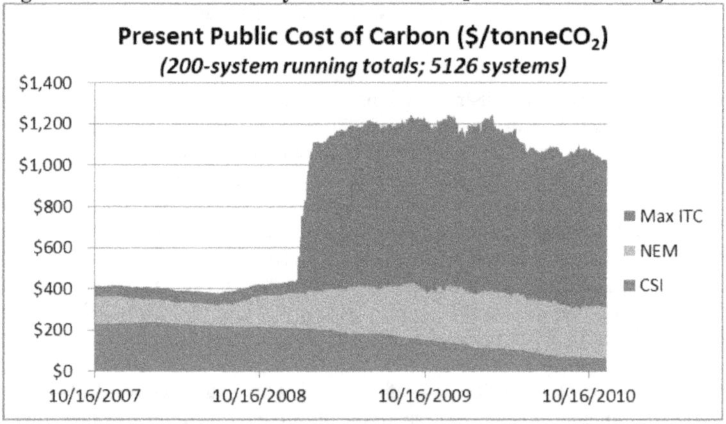


The CSI incentive is the most consistent and lowest cost of the three. For the CSI alone, carbon cost begins at $223/tonne $CO_2e$ in early 2007 and was down to $61 by December 2010. As the CSI incentive continues to decline further, thus also will its contribution to the cost of avoided carbon. In the late stages of the CSI program, then, the cost of carbon reductions fall into a realm that would likely seem reasonable to policy makers. At the end of 2010, the CSI incentive covered less than 10% of the typical PV system cost, indicating a large leverage of other funds, private and otherwise, to pay for the vast majority of the required installation costs.

Second is the NEM benefit. We have estimated this by defining the additional cost for PV-generated electricity as the difference between the pre-installation average cost of electricity for each home and a reasonable value for the avoided cost of residential PV generation. For our analysis we use 14 cents/kWh as the avoided cost. The correct number is likely between 10 and 16 cents/kWh, and our chosen value of 14 cents is an intermediate value based on several studies (Beck 2009; CPUC 2010; Yunker 2011). The NEM impact to customer and utility accrue into the future, and we therefore discount future-year avoided costs and $CO_2$ reductions to find the present value of NEM-based $CO_2$ reductions.

Quantification of the actual avoided cost to the utility for each kWh displaced by solar generation is an ongoing, multi-stakeholder process. In contrast to the CSI incentive which (by design) declines over time, the NEM benefit has grown as the CSI program has progressed and the higher tiers of energy have become more costly, as explained in Chapter 3. At a higher avoided cost, the green wedge in the figure, representing the NEM subsidy (i.e. the benefit accruing to the customer above and beyond that realized by the utility from the customer-sited generation system) would be smaller but would retain a similar shape, narrower but still growing somewhat over time as long as the current structure of NEM persists. Proper quantification of the actual costs and benefits to the grid of small-scale solar is the subject of considerable ongoing debate; as of this writing, a significant engineering-economic analysis focusing on this issue is underway under the auspices of the CPUC.

Third and final is the federal investment tax credit (ITC). The ITC is currently a large incentive for adopters, and overall it is an expensive approach to achieving carbon reductions. After the $2000 cap was lifted in January 2009, the cost per ton of $CO_2$ for the ITC went from around $65 to around $650 per tonne $CO_2e$. The per-system cost of the ITC to federal taxpayers will decline as the installed cost of PV declines, but the overall cost is dependent on the scale of the PV market going forward. As we have seen, the expansion of the ITC provided a very strong stimulus to the residential solar market; solar advocates must therefore be concerned about the consequences of its expiration in 2016. For the group of 5126 systems in our analysis, the federal solar ITC provided as much as $59M to the California economy.[26]

One potential new value stream from NEM solar is monetization of the renewable energy certificates (RECs) produced by these systems. The REC is the "renewable" attributes of the electricity produced by a renewable energy project, and can be separated from the energy itself and sold to, for example, a California utility for RPS compliance.[27]. Each kW of rooftop solar capacity produces just under 2 MWh of electricity per year, corresponding to roughly 2 RECs per year. In principle, small amounts of RECs from many systems across the region or state could be aggregated and sold in this way. It is therefore interesting to explore the underlying cost to the taxpayer and ratepayer of producing NEM-based RECs, and to compare these costs to their value in the REC marketplace.

A similar analysis to that which produced Figure 5.17 was used to calculate the cost per REC of the various incentives that accrue to NEM solar. REC production does not depend directly on the Carbon content of the displaced utility energy, but rather simply the energy (MWh) produced by each system over its lifetime. Again we see that the overall cost to the federal taxpayer increases by an order of magnitude with the raising of the ITC cap in January 2009, from $30 to over $300 per REC. The declining CSI incentive contributed the equivalent of about $30/REC by the end of 2010—down from $120/REC in 2007—while

[26] 30% of the total reported cost of $197M for these systems.

[27] One REC consists of the renewable attributes of 1 MWh of renewable electricity.

the NEM benefit costs the utility (and thus its ratepayers) roughly $100/REC. Together these incentives add up to almost $500 per REC.

**Figure 5.18. Residential PV Systems' Present Equivalent Cost of RECs**

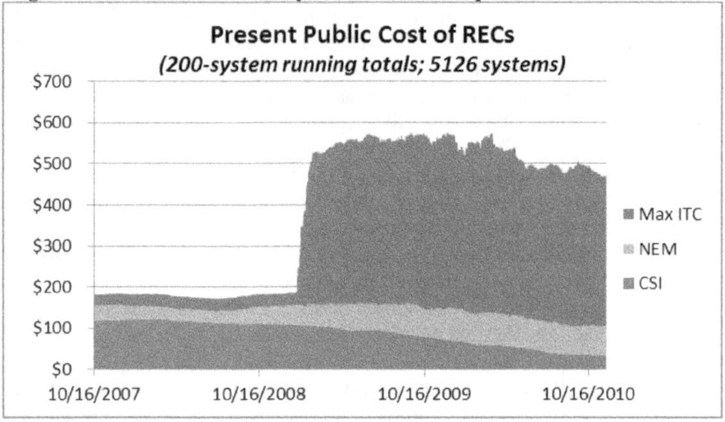


The REC market is administered by the Western Region Renewable Energy Generation Information System (WREGIS). In order for a REC to be eligible for use by a utility for RPS compliance, a REC must be certified with WREGIS, as well as meeting additional, California-specific requirements specified by the CEC. The price cap for RECs in California is $50; however, in practice the voluntary REC market has generally traded at well under $10/REC. The historical California REC price is thus 2 orders of magnitude smaller than the current set of incentives for NEM solar. We can therefore conclude that while RECs are one potential element of a plan to monetize the benefits of PV and continue the industry's profitability going forward, RECs are unlikely to generate enough cash flow to replace expiring state and federal incentives if they expire or are reformed.

### 5.5. Conclusion

In this chapter we have approached the difficult issue of measuring the takeback effect for PV adoption in the residential sector of Southern California. We developed and applied a methodology to model PV output accurately and performed the analysis for 2,410 actual systems, adding the modeled consumption to the remaining utility billed energy consumption to obtain total electricity consumption for these solar adopters. We then examined the changes in customer electricity consumption pre-installation to the post-installation period. The main conclusions are:

- The average solar customer in our study group decreases energy consumption by 3% in the first year after PV adoption.
- In subsequent years consumption rises somewhat to surpass the pre-installation year, and shows an overall increase of 2% in the third year after installation. This pattern could be seen as either a small "double-dividend" or a small takeback.

- This marginal change in consumption is much smaller than the 10-30% take-back observed by studies focusing on the energy efficiency and transportation arenas
- There is heterogeneity in the solar adopter population, making difficult the detection of specific subgroup correlations with changes in consumption. However, it is clear that increases in consumption are associated with systems sized to offset a high proportion of the customer's existing utility-provided electricity.
- Some of the heterogeneity among the adopter population can be explained by understanding the variation among the population of solar companies generating these sales. Distinct businesses models and sale approaches result in grouping of customers that correlate with pre-post behavior.
- The economics of residential PV are driven strongly by federal tax incentives and utility rate design. The NEM PV market will be negatively impacted if and when these incentives expire or are reformed. Cost reductions and new business models will be required to continue strong market expansion.

A future expanded analysis might also benefit from including behavioral information gathered through survey approaches. Variables such as leased vs. purchased systems; pre-install energy intensity (kWh/sqft); years of home ownership; and customer affluence and the actual installation of efficiency measures along with solar would shed additional light on the influences of consumption around solar adoption, and would open up the potential for targeting subpopulations of adopters for detailed analysis.

# Chapter 6. Summary of Findings and Policy Implications

## 6.1. Summary of Findings: The Solar Takeback Effect

Our consideration of consumption patterns of solar adopters has examined the specific question of a theorized "solar takeback effect." We have found that this effect is small on average, and may be different in the short and longer terms. While Kierstad's "double dividend" may be acting in the period just after PV installation, the persistence of this effect is questionable. The longer term average impact may be a small takeback, particularly for larger systems in areas with heavy cooling loads. Our basic conclusion is that energy produced by behind-the-meter solar energy systems offsets close to an equal amount of energy from the utility grid, that is, PV generation offsets utility energy by close to a 1:1 relationship. At the same time, the identified average trends mask widely variable individual responses across the range of PV adopters.

Along with the specific question of takeback, this study has sought to inform, and enable further discussion of, the question of how to design optimal solar policy as this market continues to scale up, in coordination with other efforts to reduce California's energy and carbon footprint. Primary among these, and indeed reflected in state policy through the loading order, is the imperative to achieve high levels of energy efficiency in the state's existing building stock.

In Chapter 1, this study outlined policies relevant to solar energy adoption at the federal and state levels, with a particular emphasis on California. Chapter 2 set forth a theoretical framework with a review of the literatures on the take-back effect and the diffusion of innovation. Drawing from the literature on the take-back effect in energy efficiency, a solar take-back effect was conceptualized and discussed. The innovation literature contributes a valuable perspective on what factors beyond economic factors may motivate the adoption of solar-PV.

Chapter 3 examined the economic rationale for solar adoption in the San Diego region in light of the predominant residential electricity rate structure. It also characterized the population of adopters included in terms of several relevant variables, including system size, household characteristics, assessed property value, climate zone, and customer segment. Chapter 4 analyzed the practices and trends regarding the sizing of solar systems, including the influence of the company or contractor that designs the solar system.

Together, Chapters 3 and 4 suggest that solar's innovation characteristics are relatively clear: customer familiarity and perceived relative advantage, the primary drivers of adoption, are strongly influenced by marketplace actors, central among them the sales and installation agents. However, the context in which these concepts are developed and framed for the customer vary widely; that is, the residential solar marketplace in San Diego is complex and segmented. Informational barriers for the customer introduce complexity and uncertainty. At the same time, the residential solar market is well articulated and maturing quickly.

Since the adoption decision is mediated by both the sales agent and the contractor (if different), and by the relatively obscure details of residential electric rates—which vary through time and are, in practical terms, remote from the actual consumption by the billing cycle itself—the customer virtually always lacks complete information for his or her decision making. Characterizing solar adoption as an innovation therefore depends on the characteristics and perceptions of the individual customer or appropriately segmented groups of customers.

Chapter 5 analyzed pre-and post-installation electricity data and found that the average consumption impacts of solar adoption tend to be small: around -3% (i.e. a 3% reduction) in the year immediately after installation. This effect, if it were to persist, would be the reverse of take-back, indeed something akin to Kierstead's posited "double-dividend." However, subsequent years after installation show a trend back toward pre-solar levels of consumption, with inland adopters as a whole even exceeding pre-installation levels of absolute consumption—even during relatively mild weather with lower cooling needs than in the pre-installation period. Take-back, then, where it exists, is a longer-term phenomenon with a small average net impact.

Further detailed analysis with additional independent variables might help sharpen the conclusion made here. Tracking adopters and their consumption over time would shed additional light on the dynamics of solar self-generation and overall electricity consumption, including the persistence of take-back and/or double-dividend effects in specific segments of the customer base. Matching adopters with a control group, and performing surveys to understand household-level characteristics and motivators for adoption, would enrich and deepen the current analysis.

## 6.2. POLICY IMPLICATIONS

### 6.2.1. New Incentive Models Are Necessary Moving Forward

Policy has driven, and will in all likelihood continue to influence, the scope and details of distributed solar proliferation in California. In the coming several years the policies that have most enabled the growth of the small-scale solar industry will be changing in ways that present fresh challenges for the solar industry.

First, net metering (NEM) is under some pressure due to the perception that it is significantly more expensive than other electricity procurement options, and it seems clear that California's NEM statute will be revised sooner or later. When the 5% NEM cap is approached in each IOU service territory, likely by 2014, the policy community will again be faced with defining California's rooftop PV landscape. The two general paths are (1) expand NEM past the 5% cap, which would likely be accompanied by reforms to limit its cost; and (2) develop and adopt a new approach, such as a revamped feed-in tariff (FIT) or a utility-driven procurement mechanism. It is likely that the future paths will not be nearly as advantageous for the customer or solar industry as the current NEM arrangements in the various utility territories. In both scenarios, the fact that wholesale solar energy costs have dropped to historically low levels will constitute a challenge to the small-scale solar industry. Solar providers will need both to reduce costs to the customer and to elucidate more clearly to policymakers the benefits of distributed solar energy for the robustness and stability of the utility distribution grid.

Critical to this discussion is an understanding of the value of PV to the electricity grid and utility. There are both costs and benefits of solar to the grid, and challenges for reliable integration of thee intermittent resources into the electric grid abound (Meier 2011). As of this writing, utilities and solar advocates are waging a battle over the purported cross-subsidy from non-solar to solar customers. Its outcomes—first, a CPUC technical-economic determination on whether such a cross-subsidy exists, and second, a policy/legislative decision on whether and how to limit any cross-subsidy while continuing to promote the scale-up of California solar installations—will be watershed moments for the small-scale solar industry in California.

Second, the federal ITC is set to decline from 30% to 10% on January 1, 2017. As we have seen, the ITC is by far the largest incentive for residential solar adoption. If the ITC declines, or were removed entirely, the impact on the residential solar marketplace will be negative. Again, a central question is how competitive the small-scale supply chain can become through continued maturation and strategic evolution of its business models.

Figure 3.2 showed the value opportunity opened up by the combination of NEM and the ITC. If either or both of these diminish, the value opportunity narrows considerably; whether there is a sales opportunity at all depends on the rate structures adopted in the future, which we cannot know. While marginal electric rates do not appear to motivate consumers directly (based on their consumption response), they certainly explain contractor behavior to a great extent, in that contractors in fact do utilize billing information to calculate customer benefit and size each proposed system. If, as we have seen, the most knowledgeable and highest-volume contractors continue to dominate the marketplace, we can expect this utilization of rate analysis to continue and improve. Thus the rates question is central to continued growth of the NEM solar marketplace.

Other benefits are coming to light, such as increased home value due to solar (Dastrup, Zivin et al. 2010; Hoen, Wiser et al. 2011), and due to documented "green" attributes more generally (Kok and Kahn 2012). As these benefits become more understood and accepted, they could decrease the need for strict positive economics based on the energy equation alone. Further, the increase in home value demonstrated through whole-house retrofit programs (also referred to as "building performance") and building labeling policies would likely encourage integration of solar and efficiency. The main building rating systems, including Energy Star, LEED, Green Point Rated and the California Home Energy Rating System (HERS) may provide such actionable market information. Comprehensive upgrades of existing buildings would often realize equivalent benefits at lower cost than solar alone. Certainly the benefits of improved building performance—which may, but by no means must, include solar—are myriad and include comfort, safety, noise reduction and aesthetic improvement, none of which solar alone provides.

### 6.2.2. The NEM Solar Market Requires Ongoing Oversight

As we have detailed, different contractors show distinct sizing and pricing strategies. Such differentiation is indeed a natural part of a growing marketplace. Three solar companies provide the clearest examples: those we have labeled 85, 95 and 98. The first follows a leasing approach based on sizing consciously and predictably to the tier 2-3 threshold, installing a relatively high-priced system that presumably includes in its NPV the ongoing costs of maintenance as well as margin. The second is a largely solar-as-commodity, value-oriented approach that installs high-quality systems typically sized to offset most of the customer's utility consumption. The third installs undersized, high-priced systems based on aggressive marketing techniques. These contractors are not unique, but rather demonstrate the variety of activity in an open, growing and creative marketplace.

At the same time, since both California ratepayer and federal taxpayer funds are flowing to the NEM PV marketplace, public policy should be expected to ensure that these funds are being invested effectively and accountably. The CSI has achieved accountability to a great degree; the amount and quality of publically available project data[28] is unprecedented for a program of this nature, and has enabled close scrutiny of outcomes by both regulators and industry players (CPUC 2012). This data has permitted the identification and correction of program design problems, and has allowed the CPUC and CSI program administrators to oversee participation, understand trends and, in several cases, bar unethical contractors form the program. In this way, California's program has set new standards for both rapid learning and consumer protection.

Going forward, the state depends on continued scale-up of the solar industry to reach its clean energy and carbon mitigation goals. Indeed, additional sectors of the clean energy arena, such as the nascent building performance industry, are the subject of large-scale policy initiatives. Publically-accessible program data, containing disaggregated project-level information, is essential for successful market development and transformation, especially given the anticipated decline in policy-enabled monetary resources to support the small-scale solar marketplace.

### 6.2.3. Integrate Incentive Programs for Distributed Generation, Energy Efficiency and Demand Response

Clearly, lessons from the solar industry can be applied to the energy efficiency and demand response industries. Business models that focus on the particular needs of the customer, with a minimum of confusion and maximum benefit for the customer, can grow the building performance industry. Long-term policy consistency and commitment by the legislature and regulatory agencies, equipment and installation standards, and a quality assurance program that embraces widespread availability of substantial program data will assist with development of consumer confidence, allowing the industry to scale, professionalize, and develop diverse business models based on knowledge and experience.

Over the period of study, there has been little substantive requirement for energy efficiency as a condition for receiving subsidies to install solar on existing homes. Demand response has generally not even entered this discussion. Policy efforts to link solar and efficiency have met broad resistance from the solar community, though there are signs this is changing with the growth and diversification of the solar marketplace. A number of federal, state and local programs in California have encouraged coordinated support for both energy efficiency and solar investments in existing homes. These include eligibility requirements for participation in solar incentive programs, direct subsidies for energy efficiency audits and projects, attractive financing products covering both solar and efficiency, education and outreach initiatives that support and complement private sector initiatives, and mandatory requirements such as point-of-sale efficiency disclosure and building performance standards. Of particular note are: (1) the CEC's recent adoption of the 2013 Title 24 standards, which allow solar and EE measures to be traded off for energy performance compliance in new buildings; and (2) implementation of Assembly Bill (AB) 758, which requires development of a statewide energy efficiency retrofit program for existing buildings. The present research informs the policy debates around these initiatives with its findings concerning the energy consumption behavior of solar adopters.

---

[28] Both summary and system-level CSI program data is available at www.californiasolarstatistics.com.

In general terms, the policy imperative is that the playing field for efficiency, demand response and distributed generation be level. In practical terms, this means that incentives must be aligned and coordinated to encourage integrated projects, through rate design, program support, and marketing and outreach. The same contractors, or associated complementary contractor groups, would then have an incentive to work together to offer the customer the optimal project for his or her building, rather than acting as competitors. Our state's utilities are decoupled, so that such program designs, in theory, should be possible. The challenge is to break down the silos in our regulatory agencies, utilities, and implementers so that they do not work at cross-purposes. In the new construction arena, such coordination is happening, in that both solar and above-code efficiency measures can be combined for Title 24 compliance. The retrofit arena is more difficult since the context is one of discrete projects with an initial scope of work that depend on the specifics of the situation and desires of the building owner.

We know that the smart grid reality is approaching, which opens up innumerable opportunities to easily and prospectively detect self-generation and efficiency opportunities, and to offer products to meet those needs or implement solutions that integrate well with the new electric grid. For example, inverters could utilize smart meter communication platforms to allow utility to generate ancillary services such as voltage or VAR support, power quality and the like. This approach could enable small-scale PV systems to provide added value to the grid and enhance the utility's (and ISO's) perception of the value of distributed solar.

### 6.2.4. Target Program Support to Leverage Private Financing

As we have seen, as the market grows, state, federal, and ratepayer support cannot be expected to continue at early-market-stimulus levels. Along with the benefits of NEM and the federal ITC, the CSI incentive will disappear in accordance with that program's design. At the same time, any state support, financial or otherwise, can provide a valuable endorsement to solar that is significant to contractor and customers: it gives the technology and industry a legitimacy that cannot be provided by industry alone. Further, local initiatives can provide underpinning infrastructure that private actors can leverage to reduce risk and provide long-term stability to their endeavors. For example, progressive building codes can serve to spur and educate the market to more seriously consider clean energy projects. State and local financing programs can also play a similarly important role.

In 2012, leasing and PPA models are 75% of the market (CPUC 2012). PPA provider capital is one form of financing. Other possibilities exist, and indeed could provide lower-cost solutions to the customer. For example, Property Assessed Clean Energy (PACE) programs allow local governments to form assessment districts that enable property owners to leverage real estate equity as collateral for low-cost financing for renewable energy and energy efficiency improvements on their properties. PACE programs benefit property owners by allowing them to avoid the upfront installation cost of renewable onsite generation systems and energy efficiency measures. Long-term repayment options are enabled via a lien on the property, greatly reducing the risk associated with individual creditworthiness, and opening up participation of capital markets through pooling and aggregation. Other options include so-called on-bill financing and on-bill repayment, in which the utility bill (water or electric) provides repayment security to the financier. These mechanisms are the subject of ongoing policy efforts at the California legislature and CPUC, respectively, and present promising possibilities for low-cost financing that contractors will be able to sell easily and seamlessly across the kitchen table with the customer. Such market-based facilities will be needed increasingly to permit cost-effective solar installations to continue as direct policy and program supports wane.

### 6.2.5. Reconsider RECs

The "renewable" attributes of each kWh from a certified renewable energy project can be separated from the energy itself and sold as renewable energy certificate, or RECs. Currently, in the IOU territories, the CPUC has determined that RECs produced by behind-the-meter (NEM) generation accrue to the system owner (whether the homeowner or a third party), and not the utility. In practice, third-party owners are likely to aggregate and monetize RECs, which can produce one of the many cash streams that make each project financially viable, along with accelerated depreciation, the ITC and NEM. These leasing and PPA providers also can utilize their purchasing power to achieve lower cost equipment and installation, and can customize financing to improve the LCOE of PV systems they install, and concomitantly offer improved proposals to the customer.

A robust market for solar-specific RECs, or SRECs, exists in the northeastern US. In California, a REC market does exist, but its acceptance and expansion has been hampered by delays in defining the precise nature of the necessary regulatory regime. Now that the RPS has been formalized, the REC market is a clear option for replacing at least somewhat the favorable customer economics that may disappear with reform of NEM and the decline of the ITC.

REC ownership could be one of the points of negotiation during discussions around NEM reform. Only a very small percentage of residential solar owners currently monetize their RECs. There is little practical reason for a homeowner to hold the RECs generated by her PV system, and indeed only in the IOU territories is that the case. These RECs could be assisting the utilities to comply with their RPS obligations, and thus do have at least modest value. To level the playing field between the third-party and native ownership models, access to the REC market would need to be streamlined such that individual owners have something like automatic access. Low-cost mechanisms to certify and aggregate them are not uniformly in place; automating the REC process for the smallest systems, utilizing available technology, would assist in providing access to the REC market for smaller PV customers.

The REC price in California has been consistently low, and a large pipeline of low-cost wholesale solar will likely continue to keep REC prices well below the $50 unit price cap—which itself is well below the current supports of NEM and the ITC. For example, at a REC price of $10, a typical 5kW system would produce an additional $100 per year—not enough to transform the solar transaction, but perhaps enough to provide some additional interest in the solar marketplace.

www.ingramcontent.com/pod-product-compliance
Lightning Source LLC
LaVergne TN
LVHW010736061126
851857LV00014B/1506
* 9 7 8 1 9 6 2 1 1 6 8 1 7 *